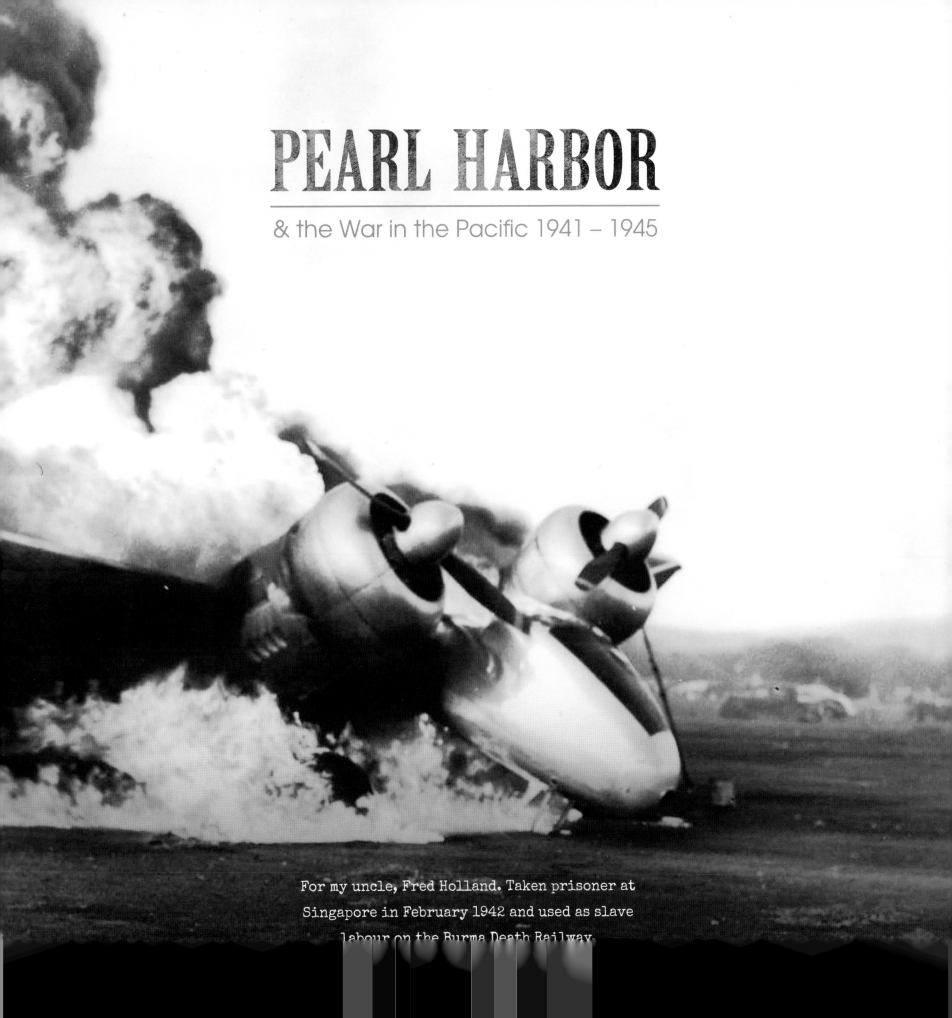

PEARL HARBOR

& the War in the Pacific 1941 – 1945

For my uncle, Fred Holland. Taken prisoner at
Singapore in February 1942 and used as slave
labour on the Burma Death Railway.

BOOKS

© Danann Publishing Limited 2016

First Published Danann Publishing Ltd 2016

WARNING: For private domestic use only, any unauthorised Copying,
hiring, lending or public performance of this book is illegal.

Photography courtesy of:
GETTY IMAGES;

Keystone-France	ullstein bild
The Asahi Shimbun	Bettmann
Roger Viollet	Time Life Pictures
MPI / Stringer	PhotoQuest
Interim Archives	Toronto Star Archives
Galerie Bilderwelt	Universal History
Hulton Archive /	Archive
Stringer	SVF2

All other images Wiki Commons

Book layout & design Darren Grice at Ctrl-d
Copy Editor Tom O'Neill

Made in EU.

CAT NO: DAN0314

ISBN: 978-0-9931813-2-0

CONTENTS

A dog thinks it is a member of the family.
To the family however, it is merely a dog

Japanese saying

The Rising Sun

ATTACK ON PEARL HARBOR

Unleashed from their aircraft carriers in the pitch black of night, 152 fighter aircraft and bombers struggled through fierce, lashing winter rain as they headed south-west. Before them lay the coast of the Hawaiian island of Oahu. The clouds parted as they climbed over the Koolau Range and suddenly there below was Pearl Harbor, basking lazily in early Sunday morning sunshine. They hit the airfields first. The fighters went for the rows of American aircraft arranged in immaculate lines, making low tight strafing runs while the dive bombers obliterated the hangars. Nothing got off the ground to oppose them. They flew on to Pearl Harbor itself, and the warships lying helpless at anchor on **'Battleship Row'**. Ship after ship was sunk, able to put up only a brief, token defence as the bombers came in for the kill. Then, as quickly as they had come, the fighters and bombers abruptly wheeled and made their escape. The date was February 7 1932.

U.S. forces in the Pacific were staging their annual Joint Army and Navy Grand Exercises. The daring – and devastating – raid on Pearl Harbor was the idea of Rear Admiral Harry E. Yarnell, staging the attack from the U.S. carriers Saratoga and Lexington. An aviator himself, Yarnell had realised that air power was soon going to challenge the traditional dominance of the battleship on the high seas. – and proved it in high style. Other admirals rushed to challenge the events they had just witnessed. They dismissed it as a fluke and the attack on Pearl Harbor was not even mentioned when the final report on the Grand Exercises was written up. Yarnell's surprise air raid was almost completely forgotten. Almost.

JAPAN IN BLOOM

Japan was sleeping when the Americans came, snuggly cocooned in its many centuries of self-imposed isolation. It still inhabited a medieval world, a world of shoguns and samurai, ronin and peasants, geisha and cherry blossom. The Americans who came were dreaming too. They dreamed of a world in which white men had a special purpose – a duty even - to shape the globe, spread western culture and bring about a new, undreamed of age through trade and commerce. It was a philosophy called **'Manifest Destiny'** and, in 1853, it had a strong grip on the presidential imagination.

Japan received a most rude and abrupt awakening when, in July that year, a small flotilla of **'Black Ships'** under the command of Commodore Matthew C. Perry slipped into Edo Bay (now Tokyo Bay) and fired a 73 gun **'salute to their own Independence Day'** to get their attention and to show just who was top dog. The Japanese immediately realised that they had nothing to match the American firepower and resorted to surrounding the Americans with tiny boats. On the deck of one, a Japanese official held up a hastily-scrawled sign saying, **'go away immediately'**. In French. The Americans didn't. They were here to talk trade - or else. Like it or not, Japan would be dragged into the 19th century. As the Japanese reluctantly acquiesced, other powers felt encouraged to turn up unannounced with their own gunboats to talk trading terms, among them the British, the Russians and the Dutch. Out of it would come The Mikado, novelty plates and the collapse of a way of life.

The Western world had hit Japan in its most vulnerable place – its pride. The nation simply could not survive such a loss of face. There were

OPPOSITE PAGE; **TOP:** Perry's visit in 1854. Lithography. 8 March 1854 **BOTTOM LEFT:** Admiral Harry Ervin Yarnel **BOTTOM MIDDLE:** Commodore Matthew Calbraith Perry **BOTTOM RIGHT:** Illustration of conference between Commodore Perry and the japanese Board 1856

insurrections, rebellions and civil wars. The shogunate fell. The feudal system collapsed. Thousands died as the country spasmed. Gradually, the modernisers began to assume power. Hundreds of western *'experts'* in everything from international banking and commerce to engineering were hired to help create a *'modern Japan'*. The Japanese people began to copy western fashions and hairstyles, while the authorities built railways and opened schools. But these modernisers were far from being liberals or laissez-faire conservatives. They wanted to build a modern Japan so that no gaijin could ever again sail into Tokyo Bay and essentially demand their surrender. Japan would be modern, because modern was strong.

Japan understood all too well that part of what made the Western powers strong was that they each had their own empires to draw from. Quite naturally, Japan wanted an empire of its own. The rapid pace of change had greatly disturbed many Japanese from deeply traditional backgrounds who responded by fuelling Japanese nationalism and declaring that the Emperor was divine. There were many *'new'* ideas in Japan that they opposed – but empire was not one of them. Japan had never been rich in either natural resources or land. All it had were fish and fault lines. Now the country found itself with a baby boom and a serious shortage of both food and space.

It was the deeply conservative military that led the way in establishing that new empire, often without government approval. In 1877 it had seized control of Hokkaido and the Ryukyu Kingdom. It waged war in China and took control of Formosa (now Taiwan) in 1895, before facing off – and defeating – Russian expansionists in the first Russo - Japanese War of 1904 – 05. In 1910 it seized Korea and its activities on the side of the Allies in World War One served more to increase its influence and

A Japanese supply train on the road between Shanghai and Nanking, 1938

territory than it did to contribute to the downfall of Germany. At war's end Japan seized both German concessions in China and German territory in the North Pacific. At the heart of the idea of empire in the Japanese sense was to take control of Asia and the Asian peoples. There seemed something right forging a mighty Asia that rejected the white imperialists – but this was not a dream of liberation or of brotherhood. The Japanese despised all non-Japanese and such an Asiatic empire could only be run by them with the other races paying tribute. They saw it perhaps as the *'Manifest Destiny'* of the Japanese people under an Emperor who was quite literally divine – a religious calling (and a civilising mission) to unite the disparate races of Asia under the holy Japanese boot.

Despite its initial successes, Japan was still hungry for more – and what lands and peoples it had consumed to date were simply not enough. In 1931, right wing forces in the military conspired to provoke an incident with the Chinese and then invaded Manchuria without the permission of their own government. When Prime Minister Tsuyoshi Inukai tried to curb the rising forces of militarism in his own country, he was swiftly murdered. Many more *'moderate'* politicians were killed too as the military increased their influence. Those in power began to see parallels with the rise of fascism in Europe – and liked what they saw. They began to reach out, forging links that would have inevitable consequences.

THE ROAD TO NANKING

By 1937, the Japanese military were eager to expand out of Manchuria and seize more territory. China at the time was a country in chaos, split between warring nationalist and communist factions, with large areas ruled over by barbarous warlords. It should surely prove no challenge to the supremely organised and disciplined Imperial Japanese Army (IJA).

The IJA manufactured an incident in Peking and then used it as a pretext to invade in force. Peking fell swiftly but as the Japanese advanced south to Shanghai, they met more determined and more skilled resistance and suffered heavy casualties. Infuriated and – quite frankly - insulted by this, the Japanese resorted to committing more and more atrocities in retaliation. When Shanghai finally fell to them in November 1937, hundreds of POWs were lined up and machine gunned in full view of the many Europeans watching helplessly from riverboats on the Yangtze.

THE RAPE OF NANKING

'I did not imagine that such cruel people existed in the modern world'

A European witness

'There were about 37 old men, old women and children. We captured them and gathered them in a square. There was a woman holding a child on her right arm... and another one on her left. We stabbed and killed them, all three – like potatoes in a skewer'

Azuma Shiro

'My men have done something very wrong and extremely regrettable'

General Iwane Matsui, Commanding Officer

The Japanese next turned their attention to Nanking, then the capital of China. They took it within just four days in December 1937, rounding up 90,000 Chinese soldiers in the process. The order was then given to kill them all. The lucky ones were simply machine-gunned.

Their prisoners now disposed of, the IJA turned their attention to the helpless civilians cowering in their homes. Japanese soldiers rampaged through the streets, looting and burning stores with their owners and families trapped inside. Crowds would be rounded up entirely at random and forced to dig their own graves before being hacked to pieces. Others were made to bury each other alive.

Virtually all foreigners had fled the city as the Japanese approached, but some twenty seven remained led by John Rabe – a German businessman working for the Siemens Company and ironically a committed member of the Nazi Party. Somehow, by some miracle, they managed to get the rampaging Japanese to respect an **'International Safety Zone'** which encompassed 2.5 square miles of the city. Here civilians would be **'off limits'** to the occupying forces. 300,000 Chinese managed to flee into the refuge. The Europeans – businessmen, missionaries, journalists, doctors in the main – then went out and somehow managed to rescue more, sometimes those under immediate threat of rape or murder. It was a magnificent stand and it revealed too that the Japanese still had some lingering fear and awe of the white man. It would not last.

The **'Rape of Nanking'** as it became known raged for almost six weeks, before finally coming to an end in February 1938. Of those who did not make it into the Safe Zone, almost everyone else died. Perhaps as many as 370,000 people were butchered. The figures are both unclear and disputed. The Japanese were not eager to keep records and those records they did keep were destroyed with great haste days before the Japanese surrender in 1945.

Accounts of atrocities were reported in the west but widely disbelieved or dismissed as propaganda. Today, the events are still denied by some Japanese, who call what went on merely **'The Nanking Incident'**. Deniers include prominent historians and politicians and any attempt to discuss them may be yet still considered in some quarters an insult to the Japanese war dead.

ABOVE: Iwane Matsui (foreground) and Prince Asaka (behind) reviewing their troops during the entrance ceremony into Nanking following its fall to the Japanese Army OPPOSITE PAGE; LEFT: Japanese tanks attacking the Gate of China MIDDLE: Head of a Chinese man, alleged to be done by the Japanese military in Nanking RIGHT: Japanese soldiers at Guanghua Gate

ABOVE: Troops of Chinese 179th Brigade departing Taiyuan, Shanxi Province **OPPOSITE PAGE; TOP LEFT:** A soldier of the IJA 4th Division firing type 92 heavy machine gun during the 1st round of Chángshā operation. Near Miluo river **TOP MIDDLE:** Civilian victims of the August 14 bombing **TOP RIGHT:** First pictures of the Japanese occupation of Peiping (Beijing) in China, on August 13, 1937 **BOTTOM:** American pro Chinese war poster

CHINA AT WAR

The Chinese called it *'The War of Resistance Against Japan'* and they'd been waging it since 1937 despite no side actually formally declaring war on the other until December 1941. The Japanese had, the year before, taken to calling it their *'holy war'*.

Since the first year which largely saw Japanese victories, the two sides had become mired down and stalemated. Hundreds of thousands died, pitched battles were won and lost on both sides but nothing changed. The Japanese held the coast and the north but could make no real progress inland, despite using poison gas on both soldiers and civilians on many hundreds of occasions.

The stalemated war was unpopular in the Japanese Home Islands, but the generals waging it were by now virtually a law unto themselves. They fought with their own government to be given ever more resources, meeting resistance from a civilian government who wished to safeguard their military and naval assets should a long anticipated war with the Soviet Union suddenly break out. When they couldn't get the troops they needed, the Japanese military in China turned to air power to break the deadlock. There were massed bomber attacks on Chinese cities, with horrendous casualties amongst the Chinese civilian population. Whole cities disappeared under the onslaught. The dead were too numerous to count. By 1940, Japan resorted to using a crude form of biological warfare against Chinese civilians, dropping bombs containing fleas infected with bubonic plague over their cities.

China somehow absorbed the punishment but could not raise the resources to fight back adequately: its aim was just to wear down, exhaust, blunt and simply outlast the Japanese. This attitude only increased when America entered the war. The Chinese now felt certain that the Japanese would lose. It was just a matter of waiting for the Americans to defeat them. They became even more entrenched, even more defensive in their strategies. They waited. 14 million Chinese would die during the long wait for an end to the conflict.

ABOVE: This terrified baby was almost the only human being left alive in Shanghai's South Station after brutal Japanese bombing. China, August 28, 1937 **OPP PAGE; BOTTOM LEFT:** Great World Amusement Center after bombing **BOTTOM MIDDLE:** Japanese troops entering Saigon (Vietnam), September 15, 1941 **BOTTOM RIGHT:** Japanese arriving at Haiphong Port, Tonkin in Indochina on September 26, 1940 **FAR RIGHT:** Shashin Shuho

PRESSURE

During the 1930s, America looked out across the Pacific with increasing alarm at Japan's ever-increasing militarism and expansionist policies. The wars in China eventually persuaded America to embark on a series of ever-more restrictive trade sanctions against Japan as well as providing financial aid to China. Japan refused to change course. Instead the nation signed a treaty with Hitler's Germany and Mussolini's Italy. The outbreak of the Second World War in Europe in September 1939 made them realise that they were being presented with a golden opportunity. As the Empire nations became ever more embroiled in war in the West, they were less able to protect their interests in the Pacific. The time, the Japanese realised, was now.

In September 1940, Japan invaded French Indochina (now Cambodia, Vietnam and Laos), sweeping aside the French Vichy regime and declaring the territory now part of a greater Asia under Japanese supervision – the **'Greater East Asia Co-prosperity Sphere'** or Daitoa Kyoueiken. America responded with even more hard-hitting sanctions, including the banning of scrap metal exports to Japan and closing the Panama Canal to their ships. Britain joined in, stopping exports of rubber from Malaya to the Japanese while the Dutch government in exile embargoed oil sales from the Dutch East Indies. Naturally Japan was gravely insulted, but its ability to wage war was also threatened. It considered seizing Malaya and the East Indies but also knew that if did so, the Americans were almost certain to take military action against them. In 1940, America had begun a huge new program of warship building. When complete, it would see the Nihon Kaigun (or Imperial Japanese Navy) dwarfed in numbers and might, and there was no way in which Japanese ship production could ever catch up again or even keep pace. The time was most definitely now. Japan started to plot.

By August 1941, America was ratcheting up the pressure on Japan again by seizing its assets and banning all exports of oil and gasoline. Given that Japan received 80% of its oil from America, it was a move that would swiftly reduce the Japanese War Machine (and indeed Japanese transport and industry) to its knees. It would have no choice but to concede the war and leave China – or to fight for new resources.

Japan and America talked. The Japanese government, seeing that things were heading invariably towards war, tried to meet some of America's demands, but its massively influential military would not let it agree to withdrawal from China. In October 1941, the relatively moderate Japanese government fell. The nation's then Army Minister, General Hideki Tojo, seized power and the military assumed responsibility for all foreign policy. Tojo proclaimed that a policy of patience and perseverance was tantamount to self-annihilation. Japan would have to fight.

By the time America's counter-proposal was received, on November 26, it was already too late. Japanese Kaigun warships had already left port bound for Pearl Harbor.

THE FIRST STRIKE

The powers that be in Japan had long decided on a bold plan of attack. They would sail south and conquer everything before them, invading the Philippines on the way and then seizing the resource-rich prizes of British Malaya and the Dutch East Indies – materials they desperately needed to wage the stalemated war in China. Once conquered, they would erect a firm defensive cordon around their new possessions and hopefully deter any attempt to dislodge them.

Simultaneously they would protect their eastern flank from any possible American intervention by attacking the U.S. Pacific Fleet at Pearl Harbor. They had noted America's stern reluctance to become embroiled in the war in Europe and misread it as weakness and lack of spine. Now, they thought, a devastating attack on Pearl Harbor could conceivably both destroy America's ability to fight in the region and any will to go to war at a single stroke. America would receive a short, sharp shock, recognise Japan's unassailable strength in the region, beg for peace and learn a lesson for its impudent opposition. There would be only a little war and everything would settle down again. This thinking was, by any stretch of the imagination, optimistic.

The details of Yarnell's surprise attack on Pearl Harbor in 1932 had

long been taught at Japanese colleges and it was decided to adopt an almost identical plan. The American Pacific Fleet – including its precious carriers – would be caught at anchor and destroyed. (There was also talk of landing invasion forces on Hawaii, but Japan simply did not have enough ships to do this and achieve its objectives to the south).

Planning began at the very start of 1941, under the control of the Harvard - educated Admiral Isoroku Yamamoto, Commander-in-Chief of the Combined Fleet. Yamamoto was not a fan of expanding the war. He could see how the IJA were struggling in China and thought that dragging in extra Western powers into the fight on the Chinese side was foolish. Still, he was a man of honour, and a man who did what he was told – and he was a great believer in the new idea that a few aircraft could sink a lot of ships. Training followed, and the Kaigun's High Command wargamed their proposed strike on Pearl Harbor. The results suggested that the U.S. Navy would lose two carriers, four battleships, three cruisers and 180 aircraft, while the Kaigun would suffer the loss only of two carriers and 127 aircraft. It sounded good. It was not until November 5 that the Emperor Hirohito gave his approval to the plan. He then gave final permission for the attack to take place on December 1.

ABOVE: Imperial Japanese Navy battleship Kirishima at Kure RIGHT: Emperor Hirohito

ABOVE: Aerial view of the U.S. Naval Operating Base, Pearl Harbor, Oahu, Hawaii, looking southwest on 30 October 1941 OPP PAGE; BOTTOM LEFT: Imperial Japanese Navy Admiral Isoroku Yamamoto (center, bending over table) with staff on battleship Nagato BOTTOM MIDDLE: United States Ambassador to Japan Joseph C. Grew BOTTOM RIGHT: Mock-up of U.S. Naval Base, Pearl Harbor, Hawaii, constructed in Japan in 1941 to help plan the attack on the installation FAR RIGHT: Propaganda poster depicting Isoroku Yamamoto

AMERICAN INTELLIGENCE

Almost as soon as Yamamoto started planning his attack on Pearl Harbor, America knew about it. Joseph C. Grew, the U.S. Ambassador to Japan, warned his superiors on January 27 that Japan would launch a surprise attack on Pearl Harbor in the event of a perceived American threat increasing. He had learned this from the Peruvian envoy to Tokyo. Somehow, that warning failed to reach the right ears or was simply not believed. American military planners firmly believed that, should war break out, it would begin with a Japanese invasion of the Philippines. They happily ignored the fact that, quite suddenly, Hawaii was awash with Japanese spies and intelligence operatives all furiously clicking away with their cameras.

Acting on Grew's intelligence was further complicated by the responsibility for Pearl Harbor's security being a military rather than naval issue. There was poor communication between the two branches of the service and, just to make matters worse, the Navy had two competing intelligence divisions of its own who were poor at sharing their resources.

More warnings were ignored: An official U.S. Navy report concluded that Pearl Harbor would be attacked, then a highly placed British spy codenamed **'Tricycle'** warned Pearl Harbor would be struck very soon. The Korean resistance claimed that they had proof that the Japanese would strike Pearl Harbor before the New Year. America itself had broken the Japanese naval codes and could hear things going on – but the information was not passed to the naval and military commanders at Pearl Harbor.

Even those who heard the warnings disregarded them or thought they were disinformation. American intelligence looked at the Japanese build up to

"I am looking forward to dictating peace to the United States in the White House at Washington"
— ADMIRAL YAMAMOTO

What do YOU say, AMERICA?

sweep south – and never dreamed that Japan could have anything like the resources needed to launch a simultaneous assault on Pearl Harbor.

BUT THEY DID.

THE KIDO BUTAI

At first, they codenamed it Operation Hawaii. Then perhaps someone realised that such a name might be too unsubtle and it was hurriedly changed to Operation Z.

Five submarines of the Imperial Japanese Navy had slipped out of Kure Naval District on November 25 1941. They would be responsible for launching the mini submarines that would take part in the attack on Pearl Harbor. Within a day, six Japanese aircraft carriers chosen to take part in the attack – the Akagi, Kaga, Sōryū, Hiryū, Shōkaku, and Zuikaku - would also set sail with 350 aircraft on board, this time from Hitokkapu Bay. Joining them were the battleships Hiei and Kirishima, the heavy cruisers Tone and Chikuma and nine destroyers - the Isokaze, Urakaze, Tanikaze, Hamakaze, Arare, Kasumi, Kagero, Shiranuhi, and Akigumo. Together they would comprise the Kidō Butai – the Striking Force – under the command of Vice Admiral Chuichi Nagumo. It was, by far, the most powerful carrier task force ever assembled.

The Kidō Butai moved west fast and it moved sure, doing everything it could to hide itself. Ahead steamed an innocent-looking civilian Japanese passenger liner, reporting back constantly to affirm that no American ships were about. By the early hours of December 7 1941, they had sailed 3,300 sea miles and were undetected and in position. The first wave of Kaigun bombers and fighters lifted off the flight deck at 06.10am, into fierce 40 foot waves that lashed the decks beneath their undercarriages...

THE CARRIERS LEAVE

Before the Japanese set off for Pearl Harbor, they had been told that the American aircraft carriers were their main target. By extreme good fortune (for the Americans), all three of the carriers belonging to the Pacific Fleet had left harbor while the Japanese force was in transit. The Enterprise had been the first to leave, ferrying aircraft to Wake Island to bolster its defences. The Lexington had left on December 5 bound for Midway, again to deliver aircraft, and Saratoga had returned to America for repairs at Puget Sound dockyards. Indeed, a full third of all American warships in the Pacific Fleet were out at sea that day, fuelling later conspiracy theories that Roosevelt did indeed have advanced warning of the attack and saved as many of his fighting assets as he could.

LEFT: Chuichi Nagumo MIDDLE: Imperial Japanese Navy aircraft carrier Zuikaku at Hitokappu Bay prior to sortieing to attack Pearl Harbor
RIGHT: Nakajima B5N aircrews pose in front of one of their aircraft on the Imperial Japanese Navy aircraft carrier Kaga the day before Pearl Harbor

LEFT: Japanese Navy Aichi D3A1 Type 99 carrier bombers prepare to take off from an aircraft carrier during the morning of 7 December 1941
MIDDLE: Japanese aircraft carrier Akagi **RIGHT:** Aircraft carriers USS Lexington (CV-2) and Saratoga (CV-3) at the yard **TOP:** USS Enterprise (CV-6) moored at Ford Island, Pearl Harbor

Tora! Tora! Tora!

ATTACK ON MALAYA

Pearl Harbor did not see the opening shots of the Pacific War. The first Japanese attack on Allied territory actually came in Malaya, just after midnight on December 8 1941. Across the international date line, in Hawaii it was December 7 – and Japanese warplanes were still about an hour and twenty minutes out from a slumbering Pearl Harbor.

Indian soldiers at Kota Bharu spotted Japanese transport ships just offshore disgorging landing craft filled with over 5,000 Japanese troops of the 25th Army. As they came ashore, the Indians hammered them with machine gun fire and directed British howitzers down onto the stretch of beach. The first wave of Japanese became pinned down, as did the wave following them in. Both suffered heavy casualties. Lockheed Hudsons of the Royal Australian Air Force then began bombing both the beaches and the transport ships at anchor out in the ocean. Despite this, by 10am, the Japanese had taken control of the beachhead by sheer force of numbers. A Commonwealth counter-attack half an hour later only partially succeeded and the Japanese fought off further actions. By the next day, they had surged inland, forcing Commonwealth forces into retreat and seizing the local town and its airport. Some 300 Japanese soldiers were killed in the action and a further 500 wounded.

The British High Command had been anticipating a possible Japanese attack for months if not years, but could not muster the nerve for launching a pre-emptive strike against the Japanese troops they had spotted mustering in French Indochina. Some thought the Japanese were trying to provoke them into firing the first shot so that they could claim the British started the war.

At 4am on December 8, seventeen Japanese Nell bombers out of Saigon bombed Singapore, killing 61 people - most of them Ghurkha troops. The island's defenders responded with fierce fire from anti-aircraft batteries and the guns of the battleship Prince of Wales and battlecruiser Repulse joined in – but no enemy aircraft were hit, even though it was a bright moonlit night.

PEARL HARBOR

'We won a great tactical victory at Pearl Harbor and thereby lost the war.'

Captain Tadaichi Hara

At quarter to three in the morning of December 7, a patrolling U.S. Minesweeper, the Condor spotted a submarine periscope less than 2 miles southwest of the entrance to Pearl Harbor. Knowing that no friendly subs were in the area, she sent an alert to the Ward, a U.S. destroyer close by. A further alert was issued by the supply ship USS Antares. By 06.45, the Ward made contact with a submarine and sank it with 4 inch gunfire and then a pattern of depth charges as it dived to get away. A PBY flying boat joined in the attack. (This may or may not have been the same vessel spotted earlier by the Condor as five different midget submarines were all trying to infiltrate the harbor at this time). Within minutes, they alerted Pearl Harbor to the clash. The message did reach the Naval Commander of Pearl Harbor Admiral Husband Kimmel himself but – having been made cynical by the sheer number of false reports of submarine sightings in recent months - he ignored it pending verification.

The Army's new Opana Mobile Radar Station then picked up incoming aircraft at 07.02. Although inexperienced, the operators made the signal out to be fifty or more aircraft inbound for Oahu. They phoned in to their superior, himself a radar trainee. He concluded the

Tora! Tora! Tora!

ABOVE: Students of the Sasebo Imperial Japanese Navy School in training on September 17, 1941 in Sasabo, Nagasaki, Japan

blips were actually a flight of friendly B-17 bombers due to arrive in secret that morning and told the anxious radio operators *'don't worry about it'*. There were other frantic scrambled calls from civilian planes up over the island that morning, as they were engaged and shot down by Japanese fighters sweeping across the landscape – but nothing that made sense. At the very same time, the Ward was responding to another submarine contact with depth charges…

At 07.48, Kaneohe Naval Air Station was struck. Its entire fleet of 33 PBY Catalina flying boats were all wiped out by the end of the morning's events. At 07.53, Commander Fuchida sent the message *'Tora! Tora! Tora!'* It meant *'Surprise Attack'* but was also a play on the Japanese word for Tiger. They had achieved complete surprise.

At 07.55, Commander Logan C. Ramsey was in his office at the Command Centre on Ford Island Naval Station when, out of the window he saw a low flying aircraft dropping a bomb. As everything exploded around him he ran to the radio room and frantically dictated a stark, uncoded message to his radio operator. It went out to every ship and every base:

AIR RAID ON PEARL HARBOR X
THIS IS NOT A DRILL.

At the same time as Ford Island was being attacked, Zero fighters and Val dive bombers struck the Army Air Force base at Fort Wheeler, Kaneohe Naval Air Station, Ewa Field, John Rodgers Field and Hickam Field, catching all the aircraft on the ground neatly lined up in rows on the flight line. The dive bombers concentrated on the hangars, mostly with incendiary bombs, while the Zeros swooped down almost to treetop height and strafed the lines of aircraft. At Hickam, there was a direct hit on the mess hall, killing 35 U.S. servicemen as they sat down for breakfast. Adding to the chaos, it was now that the secret flight of American B-17s arrived and prepared to land. They carried no guns and could only desperately buck and weave as the Japanese fighters went after them. Most escaped and managed to make emergency landings at Hickam Field at the height of the raid, one coming down on a nearby golf course.

Now the Japanese attention turned to Battleship Row. There were

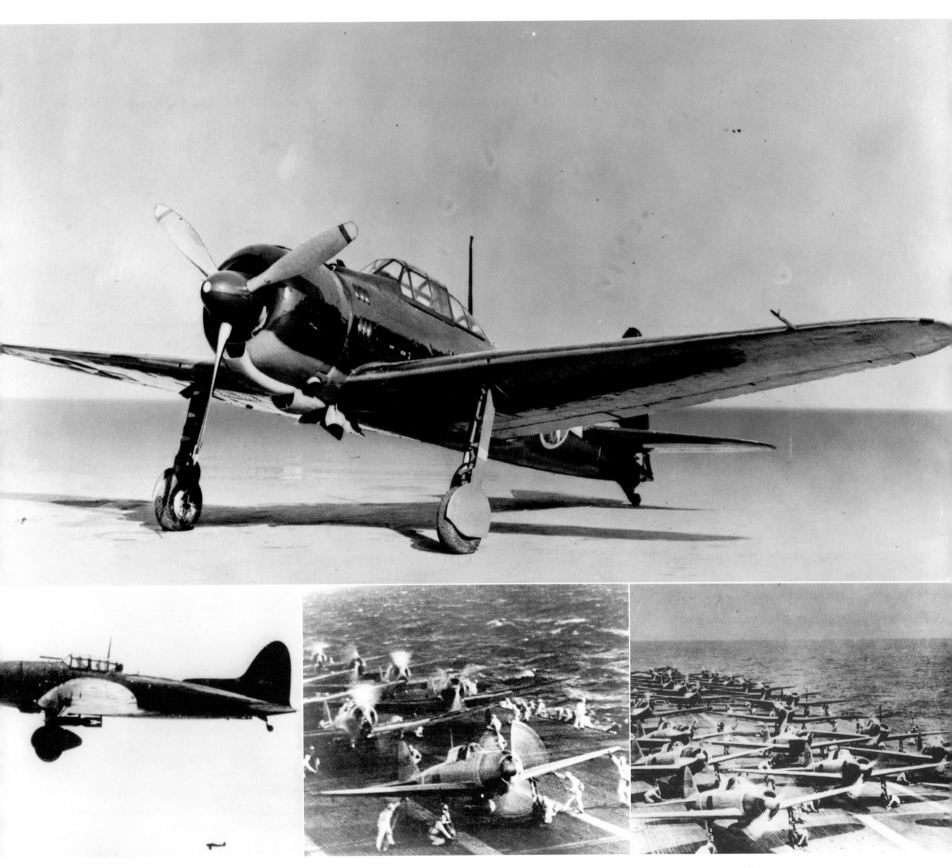

OPPOSITE PAGE: Japanese aviators some time before the bombing of Pearl Harbor **TOP:** Mitsubishi, A6M, Zero Fighter **LEFT:** Imperial Japanese Navy Aichi D3A2 "Val" dive bombers in flight **MIDDLE & RIGHT:** Japanese naval aircraft prepare to take off from aircraft carrier Shokaku to attack Pearl Harbor

approximately 100 U.S. warships at anchor in the harbor that morning, a mixture of battleships, destroyers, cruisers and support vessels. The slower, more cumbersome Kate torpedo bombers came in first, making simultaneous attack runs from east and west with Mark 91 torpedoes especially adapted for the relative shallow waters of Pearl Harbor. The first ships to be hit were the light cruiser Helena and the minelayer Oglala. Both were crippled. The battleship Utah took two torpedoes and capsized within minutes, killing 64 officers and crew.

Two torpedoes struck the battleship USS California , another two the battleship Arizona and a fifth hit the battleship Nevada as it tried to fend off the torpedo bombers with ferocious machine gun fire. Its port bow was torn clean open. Right in the centre of Battleship Row both the battleships USS Oklahoma and West Virginia received multiple torpedo strikes and had their hulls torn open. Such was the speed of the attack that the crew of the Oklahoma were still struggling to action stations when the order was given to abandon ship. She heeled over and as desperate men tried to get off her listing hull, another torpedo hit home. 415 men died on the Oklahoma – but 32 were later rescued after being trapped inside her hull for two days.

The regular high level Kate bombers came in next, dropping their 800kg armour-piercing ordnance from 10,000 feet. At 8.04, the Arizona was hit on the forward deck by an armour piercing bomb. It exploded next to the forward ammunition magazine and over a million pounds of stored gunpowder went up with it, creating a huge fireball. A witness to the cataclysm said the whole battleship jumped twenty feet out of the water and then broke almost in two. It sank in just nine minutes, taking 1,177 men with it – almost half of all those who died at Pearl Harbor that

ABOVE: U.S. Navy sailors in a motor launch rescue a survivor from the water alongside the sunken battleship USS West Virginia OPPOSITE PAGE; TOP: Postcard made to enhance the " Tripartite Pact " between Italy , Germany and Japan BOTTOM LEFT: The USS West Virginia (sunken at left) and USS Tennessee (BB-43) shrouded in smoke BOTTOM MIDDLE: Battleship Row, The capsized battleship USS Oklahoma is visible in the center BOTTOM RIGHT: Crew abandoning the USS California as burning oil drifts down on the ship

day. Now the West Virginia started to go down, settling on the bottom with its gun turrets just above water as a combination of torpedoes and bombs proved just too much for her. 105 men would die on the Oklahoma – some of them trapped helplessly inside her hull and beyond rescue. (They are believed to have finally perished just before Christmas Eve.)

Seven minutes after the Arizona was hit, the destroyer Helm was frantically trying to escape into the open seas when it spotted a Japanese mini-sub stuck fast on a reef. It opened fire and missed. The submarine shook itself free, tried to dive and then became snagged again. The crew fled. One drowned. The other was to become the first Japanese prisoner of war of the conflict. As it too tried to escape, the destroyer Monaghan received a warning from another ship that they had spotted a mini-sub. Sighting the sub too, The Monaghan engaged. The midget sub fired a torpedo at the Monaghan but it streaked past harmlessly as the Monaghan came on at the sub with its guns blazing then rammed it at full speed before dropping depth charges at virtually point blank range. The mini-sub rapidly sank to the bottom.

The first wave of raiders withdrew at 08.30am. The second wave came in a fraction before 9am, launching fresh air attacks on Kaneohe, Bellows Field, Hickam Field, Wheeler Field and Ewa Mooring Mast Field. By now, several U.S. fighters had managed to take off and intercepted the fresh wave of Japanese raiders. Army fliers second lieutenants George S. Welch and Kenneth Taylor had managed to get airborne in their Curtiss P-40 Tomahawk fighters from their base at Haleiwa and were officially credited with shooting down four Japanese warplanes during the first wave. They returned to rearm and refuel and, despite

Taylor being wounded and Welch having some guns jammed, they went straight back up after the next wave, accounting for another three Japanese aircraft. (Welch was later recommended for the Medal of Honor for his bravery, but it was denied to him when his commanding officer complained he had taken off without permission).

By the time the second wave of Japanese aircraft arrived over Battleship Row, American defences were ready and it met with a furious, thick barrage of anti-aircraft fire. Now dive bombers rather than torpedo planes were the favoured method of attack. Japanese bombers struck the naval yard's dry dock and damaged the battleship Pennsylvania. The destroyers Cassin and Downes were also in for repairs. Bombs struck the oil tanks between the two ships and triggered an on-board ammunition explosion. The Cassin rolled off her blocks and toppled on top of the Downes. More bombers went after the fleeing battleship Nevada, trying to sink her in the entrance to the harbor and thereby stop any other ships escaping. Rather than let that happen, her Captain took the decision to run her aground where the ship would be no obstruction. At 9.30am, the destroyer Shaw was consumed by a huge explosion which blew her bow clean off. The light cruiser Raleigh had a miraculous escape when a falling bomb missed the ship's full fuel tanks by just 10 feet.

By 10am, the Japanese raiders were on their way back to their carriers. They were exultant when they landed and shouted for a third wave of attacks to commence. They were overruled. Japanese commanders understood that the element of surprise had been lost and that it was the second wave that had borne the largest share of the casualties. A third wave would be flying straight into the sights of thousands of guns.

ABOVE: Heavily damaged Hangar No. 11 at Hickam Field. In front is the tail of a damaged Douglas B-18 Bolo bomber from the 18th Bombardment Group OPP. PAGE; BOTTOM LEFT: Japanese Navy Nakajima B5N2 torpedo plane from the aircraft carrier Zuikaku over Hickam field BOTTOM MIDDLE: Burned-out wreckage of a Curtiss P-40 pursuit aircraft, near Hangar 4 at Wheeler Army Airfield BOTTOM MIDDLE: Planes and hangars burning at Wheeler Field

There was another reason that commanders chose to end the attack. No one had seen the American carriers in the harbor. The prime targets of the whole raid were out at sea, safe. By 1pm, the Kidō Butai had turned and was already sailing for home. They had lost 29 aircraft and – they later discovered – five of their mini-subs. A further 20 aircraft were later scrapped or pushed overboard because of the battle damage they had sustained.

Behind them, the Americans gradually took stock of the situation. Five of the eight U.S. battleships in the harbor had been sunk or were heavily damaged, as were eight other fighting ships. 188 aircraft had been destroyed and a further 150 damaged, the overwhelming majority still while on the ground. 2,400 people had been killed. Almost immediately, the Navy tried to launch a counter attack with the carrier USS Enterprise sent on an intercept. Unfortunately, the Navy had no idea where the Japanese carrier fleet was and the Enterprise was despatched in completely the opposite direction. Tragically, just before 9 0'clock that night, a flight of six Wildcat fighters from the Enterprise were shot at by friendly fire as they tried to land on Ford Island. Only one aircraft survived.

One Japanese prisoner was taken - Ensign Sakamaki Kazuo, a crewman from one of the mini-subs. (When Admiral Yamamoto heard of this later, he is described by witnesses as having nothing less than a temper tantrum, quite literally balling his fists and stamping his feet and screaming that the wretched man had defiled the honour of the Kaigun and Japan itself).

ABOVE: USS Nevada on fire in Pearl Harbour **OPP. PAGE; TOP LEFT:** Hickam Air Base during the Japanese attack. A camouflaged Boeing B-17E Flying Fortress is in the foreground, a silver B-17D is visible in the background **TOP MIDDLE:** The Japanese "Type A" midget submarine HA-19 partially hauled up on eastern Oahu beach, during salvage by U.S. forces **TOP RIGHT:** The first Japanese POW Kazuo Sakamaki

ABOVE: The battleship USS California sinks near Ford Island after the Japanese bombed and torpedoed the ship during the attack

OPPOSITE PAGE; The battleship USS Pennsylvania (center right), sits in drydock at Pearl Harbor, amid the ruins of the USS Cassin and USS Downes

ABOVE & OPPOSITE PAGE: Photographs of salvage operations at Pearl Harbor Naval Shipyard taken by the shipyard during the period following the Japanese attack

ABOVE: Men of the Naval Air Station at Kaneohe, Hawaii, place leis on the graves of their comrades killed in the Japanese attack **OPPOSITE PAGE;**
The body of a Japanese Lieutenant who crashed during the attack on Pearl Harbor, is buried with military honors by U.S. troops

ATTACK ON THE PHILIPPINES

Just ten hours after attacking Pearl Harbor, Japanese warplanes from Formosa (now Taiwan) were bombing the Philippines in preparation for an invasion. The Japanese had no particular interest in the islands, except to use them as a staging post for an assault on the oil-rich Dutch East Indies and to prevent the Americans using the islands to block their ambitions and lines of communication back to the Home Islands.

Despite the fact that the American commander in the Philippines, General Douglas MacArthur, knew full well what had happened at Pearl Harbor and also that enemy forces were on the way, the Americans were woefully unprepared. There had been firm plans in place to launch a pre-emptive strike against Japanese airfields on Formosa with flights of B-17 Flying Fortresses, but MacArthur hesitated. He did not want to launch the first strike from the Philippines – and so the Japanese raiders came over unopposed.

At Clark Field, 50 miles north of the capital Manila, the Japanese caught both American Army fighters and bombers on the ground. 15 B-17s and 34 P-40E fighters were destroyed or seriously damaged and 55 men killed. Iba, an important fighter base on Luzon lost all but two of its P-40s. Another 21 servicemen died. By the end of the day, half of all American warplanes on the islands were lost – aircraft that were essential not only for the defence of the islands but also to provide cover for American warships in the area. Ports and cities were also bombed.

TOP: General Douglas MacArthur **ABOVE LEFT;** General MacArthur with Maj. Gen. Jonathan M. Wainwright in the Philippines **ABOVE MIDDLE;** Aftermath of the Japanese attack on Clark Field on December 8, 1941 **ABOVE RIGHT;** A burning building along Taft Avenue which was hit during the Japanese air raid in Barrio, Paranaque, December 13, 1941, the Philippine Islands.

THE JAPANESE STRIKES CONTINUE

Shortly after news of Pearl Harbor broke, eight Japanese bombers raided the Cable Station and Pan-American compound on Guam in the Marianas Islands, as well as numerous other targets and the minesweeper USS Penguin was sunk. 36 G3M3 Nell medium bombers out of the Marshall Islands attacked Wake Island. They destroyed eight U.S. Marine Corps Wildcat fighters caught on the ground and killed 23 men. Shortly after, it was Hong Kong's turn to be hit, at first from the air before Japanese military units started their invasion. In mainland China, more ground forces meanwhile began their invasion of Shanghai. They met with no opposition.

SNEAK ATTACK

The raid on Pearl Harbor – although it was meant to come as a surprise was never intended as a 'sneak attack'. Japan would declare war on America just before it began. Only it didn't. The Japanese Ministry of Foreign Affairs had only learned about the plan a few days before, and were confused about their role. The declaration of war was sent to the Japanese Embassy in Washington in 14 separate encrypted parts. The staff, not realising the urgency of the messages, simply took too long to decode and translate them into English. By the time American Secretary of State Cordell Hull, received the document from Ambassador Nomura, the first wave of Japanese aircraft had already struck and were returning to their carriers…

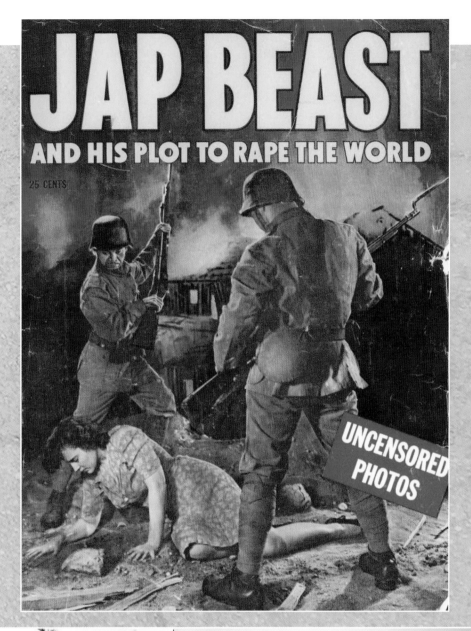

TOP: American anti-Japanese propaganda magazine depicting Japan's brutality ABOVE LEFT; G3M Type 96 Attack Bomber Nell ABOVE MIDDLE; Two U.S. Marine Corps Grumman F4F-4 Wildcat fighters at Henderson Field, Guadalcanal, Solomon Islands ABOVE RIGHT; Japanese Embassy, Washington

AMERICA REACTS

President Theodore Roosevelt was having a conference with his advisor Harry Hopkins when he was first told about Pearl Harbor. His Navy Secretary Frank Knox burst into the room and gabbled the news. It was 1.30pm in Washington DC. Throughout the day, the President went about his work with a *'deadly calm'* and later that night hosted a meeting with his Cabinet in which he told them,' ***this is probably the most serious crisis any Cabinet has confronted since the Civil War.'*** By now he had received more explicit details of the attack and was described as being *'visibly distraught'* about what had gone on, especially the machine gunning of helpless sailors in the water by Japanese fighter planes.

The next day, Roosevelt addressed Congress and told them that December 7 1941 was a *'date that would live in infamy'*. He then asked for permission to declare war on Japan. Approval was almost unanimous. This was just one holdout. On December 11, Germany and Italy formally declared war on America. If there were any doubts before, now there were none. This was a world war.

By December 22, British Prime Minister Winston Churchill had arrived in Washington to express solidarity and to plan a way forward. Churchill stayed as a guest in the White House, horrifying everyone by his habit of wandering around the building in the dead of night either in just his underwear or else stark naked. His speech to Congress, given on Boxing Day 1941, was more popular. He talked of partnership – and

parentage, reminding the Congressmen that he was indeed half-American himself – and it was a triumph. The standing ovation was deafening and seemed to go on forever. He then had lunch with Congress, returned to the White House and promptly had his first heart attack. It was kept very secret.

THE VOTE

On December 10 1941, the Japanese Cabinet put to the vote what to call their splendidly lucky new conflict. They settled on *'The Greater East Asia War'* and two days later told the Japanese nation that it was a war of independence by all asian people against the whites.

FAILURE AT PEARL HARBOR

'When this war is over, the Japanese language will be spoken only in Hell.'

Admiral William Halsey, December 7 1941

Although it did not seem so to either the Americans or the Japanese in December 1941, the raid on Pearl Harbor was actually a failure. The main target of the Japanese attack at Pearl Harbor had been the three American carriers. They had missed all of them. Secondly, they had done relatively little damage to the infrastructure, which included vast fuel depots and dockyard facilities which would prove most useful in the years to come. Thirdly, the Americans eventually managed to salvage many of the warships sunk at Pearl Harbor and reuse them in the war effort.

Lastly, the Japanese seriously believed that – as good capitalists – the Americans would see no profit in going to war. They would accept things. What they could not foresee was that, within bare weeks, all good Americans would be singing the hastily written propaganda song

'We're gonna have to slap the dirty little Jap':

We're gonna have to slap the dirty little Jap
And Uncle Sam's the guy who can do it
We'll skin the streak of yellow from this sneaky little fellow
And he'll think a cyclone hit him when he's thru it!

'**Remember Pearl Harbor**' was a resounding patriotic rallying cry. Three months later, all Japanese Americans were told to submit themselves for internment. America was serious.

THE FALL OF GUAM

Guam, the southernmost of the Marianas Islands (and the only island of any significance there not already occupied by the Japanese), was defended by little more than a lightly armed token force – but the Japanese didn't know that. Instead, they assembled a huge flotilla of four heavy cruisers, four destroyers, two gunboats, six submarine chasers and two minesweepers to take it. On December 10 1941, 6,000 Japanese troops stormed ashore on two separate beachheads. It was all over by the early hours of the next day. The size of the attack was so overwhelming that casualties were light. Just one Japanese soldier was killed. Guam was the first American soil to fall to the Japanese.

THE SINKING OF FORCE Z

As the Japanese consolidated their beachhead on the north east coast of Malaya, they faced a significant threat from Royal Navy forces in the area.

Task Force Z had been put together specifically to counter the threat of possible Japanese aggression in the region. It consisted of the battleship HMS Prince of Wales, the battlecruiser HMS Repulse and four destroyers. It was meant to have an aircraft carrier to provide air cover, but the ship designated for the task, HMS Indomitable, had accidentally run itself aground during sea trials in the Caribbean and was unavailable for service.

On December 10 1941, while sailing down the East coast of Malaya heading into Singapore, the force was caught by Japanese aircraft. Rather than electing to liaise with aircraft cover from Allied airfields along the way, its commanders had chosen to maintain strict radio silence and try to sneak back to port.

Eight Nell bombers attacked first, concentrating on the Repulse but scoring just one hit and causing only light damage. In turn five of the bombers were hit and either damaged or destroyed by fierce anti-aircraft fire from the battlecruiser. Half an hour later, a second wave of 17 Nells – this time armed with torpedoes – swept in on the ships. Eight went after the Repulse while nine engaged the Prince of Wales. All the torpedoes missed – except one. The sole torpedo to strike home hit the propeller shaft area of the Prince of Wales. Water flooded in and the ship developed a dangerous list which meant all the anti-aircraft guns along her port side couldn't sufficiently elevate to bring to bear on any attacker. Power was lost to some more guns to starboard. Electrical systems started to fail, hampering on board communications. The crew now struggled just to steer, and her speed dropped to 15 knots. A flight of Bettys turned up half an hour later, slamming three more torpedoes into her starboard side.

While HMS Prince of Wales was fighting for her life, the Repulse was subjected to torpedo attacks from port and starboard simultaneously. She was hit four times and the call came to abandon ship. The stricken battlecruiser at first listed to port before rolling and sinking. Just ten minutes later, HMS Prince of Wales took a direct hit from a bomb which penetrated the upper decks and exploded amongst the wounded huddled down below. As the great battleship began to sink, the destroyer HMS Express pulled alongside in a desperate race to take on board survivors. Meanwhile the destroyers Electra and Vampire worked to pull the survivors of the Repulse from the sea.

It was one of the worst disasters ever experienced by the Royal Navy. 513 men went down with the Repulse and a further 327 were lost from the Prince of Wales. Winston Churchill was later to write, '*In all the war, I never received a more direct shock.... Over all this vast expanse of waters Japan was supreme, and we everywhere were weak and naked.*'

THE FALL OF WAKE ISLAND

The Japanese launched their invasion of Wake Island on December 11 1941, committing 450 elite troops supported by light cruisers and destroyers. Coastal defences accounted for one of the destroyers while the second was sunk by the island's four remaining Wildcats. Both Kaigun ships exploded and were lost with all hands on board. Panicked by the fiercer than expected resistance, the Japanese called off their assault and retreated out to sea.

Bombing raids on the island continued, and when the Japanese returned on December 23 they supported the assault this time with two aircraft carriers, both fresh from the Pearl Harbor raid, as well as two heavy cruisers. 1500 Japanese marines were thrown on to the beaches and simply overwhelmed the defenders in a day. Some 49 U.S. Marines died in the fighting, compared with 850 Japanese dead over the fifteen days of attacks on the island. Now in command, the Japanese quickly built up their own formidable coastal defences, using captured Americans as slave labour.

OPPOSITE PAGE: Sinking of the battleship 'HMS Prince of Wales' (back) and of the battlecruiser 'HMS Repulse' (front) after being hit by Japanese torpedo aircrafts off the Malaysian coast near Kuantan

BLACK CHRISTMAS - THE FALL OF HONG KONG

'If Japan goes to war there is not the slightest chance of holding Hong Kong or relieving it,' Winston Churchill had noted back in January of 1941. *'I wish we had fewer troops there, but to move any would be noticeable and dangerous.'*

Japanese troops had first entered the territory of Hong Kong on December 8 1941, greatly outnumbering the defending forces. After four days of intense fighting, they had effectively seized the mainland and Commonwealth forces retreated to Hong Kong Island. By December 15, Japan had begun a sustained bombardment of the island and was making repeated demands for the garrison to surrender. When this was refused, they began shipping troops across the harbor to the island using captured junks and sampans on the night of December 18. Within a day, the Japanese were in control of a large part of the island. A counter-attack failed and resistance was undermined by a lack of both ammunition and fresh water. As the Allies were pushed back, exultant Japanese troops went on an orgy of looting, raping and killing. It's estimated that as many as 10,000 Chinese women were raped in just the first few days.

On Christmas morning, the Japanese fell upon St. Stephen's College Emergency Hospital where wounded Commonwealth soldiers were trapped. Two doctors carrying a white flag approached the Japanese. They were the first victims, shot and then bayoneted on the ground. 170 soldiers and nursing staff were then systematically butchered. At least seventy of the helpless soldiers were bayoneted in their beds or impaled on Japanese swords. They raped the nurses and then murdered most of them. Survivors were taken captive and later used in Japanese military brothels on the island. Incredibly some patients did survive, hastily bundled into cupboards or laundry baskets and hidden by their nurses and doctors as the Japanese approached.

The Governor of Hong Kong, Sir Mark Aitchison Young, formally surrendered to the Japanese forces on the afternoon of Christmas Day, 1941. 4,500 British and Commonwealth troops died in the defence of the island, while the Japanese lost 2,750 men. 6,500 Allied prisoners of war were taken. Thousands of them would die in captivity. At least 10,000 Hong Kong Chinese were executed by the Japanese in the long wait for freedom, and often on the flimsiest of pretexts. 70 were murdered after the Japanese surrender in 1945.

MAIN IMAGE: Japanese Infantry penetrating into Hong Kong passing by burning petrol depots **BOTTOM LEFT:** Japanese Army crossing the border between Hong Kong and mainland, 1941 **BOTTOM MIDDLE:** Japanese Army crossing the Kwong Fuk Bridge near Tai Po Market, 1941 **BOTTOM RIGHT:** Japanese Army assault on Tsim Sha Tsui Station, 1941

THE FALL OF THE PHILIPPINES

General MacArthur had asked for 400,000 troops to adequately defend the Philippines. By the time the Japanese came, he could barely muster 130,000, few of whom were adequately trained or spoke enough English to understand their officers. With over seventy different dialects spoken on the islands, they could not even understand each other on occasions. They were short of artillery and rifles.

The Japanese invasion began with a landing on Batan Island on December 8. Two days later, more soldiers streamed ashore on Camiguin Island and on Northern Luzon, where the landings and the support ships were bombed unsuccessfully by B-17s. Two days later, there were unopposed landings in Southern Luzon and the first Japanese came ashore on Mindanao on December 19. By now, Admiral Hart had taken the strategic decision to withdraw most of the U.S. Asiatic Fleet away from the islands because of increasing Japanese air superiority and so there was little that could effectively stand in the way when 43,000 Japanese soldiers supported by 90 tanks began their landings all along the east coast of Lingayen Gulf. A handful of B-17s tried to stop them gaining a fast, firm foothold but they were largely ineffectual, as were Allied units under General Wainwright who tried and failed to hold them on the beaches. 7,000 more Japanese soldiers stormed ashore the following day on Luzon and here too Allied attempts to stop them ended in total failure as they broke through and started to surge towards the Philippines capital Manila.

By Christmas Eve 1941, MacArthur had no choice but to implement a pre-war plan to pull his forces back to the mountainous Bataan Peninsula, which was being frantically fortified and resupplied even as MacArthur's men streamed back. The plan called for them to hold fast and await reinforcements. No reinforcements would ever come.

By mid-January 1942, the Japanese considered the American and Filipino forces effectively bottled up. They withdrew their best troops for use elsewhere and replaced them with inferior forces, whilst also withdrawing a good percentage of their air capability for use in the Dutch East Indies. This strategic error prolonged the fighting for four more months and resulted in heavy Japanese battle casualties once the offensive on the Bataan Peninsula recommenced.

MacArthur himself had been ordered out of the theatre on 22nd February and he had shipped out to Australia where he made the solemn promise, *'I shall return'* and promptly received the Congressional Medal of Honor. Behind him, the soldiers he left behind composed their own words of defiance. They sang:

'We are the battling bastards of Bataan. No papa, no mama, no Uncle Sam'

They fought like fury in the worst of conditions and, by mid-February, the Japanese were brought to a standstill and had to call in reinforcements from China. Now facing fresh troops spearheading the assault against them, the Allied forces were progressively pushed back or rolled up. Supplies were short and exhausted men were forced to march or fight on a minimum number of calories a day. Heat and disease, including malaria and dysentery, reduced much of the fighting force to a state of near collapse. Fighting ceased and surrender came on April 9 1942.

Now, just 11,000 men made what was almost a last stand on the island fortress of Corregidor, a U.S. Army artillery position on the entrance to Manila Bay. The end finally came when two Japanese divisions assaulted the position and drove the defenders into a small, unsustainable pocket. The senior American officer left on the islands, General Wainwright, asked for surrender terms on May 6.

Although Japan had now effectively conquered the Philippines, it never gained anything like full control over the islands. Filipinos and American soldiers separated from their units waged a fierce guerrilla war on the occupiers from the mountains and jungle and denied the Japanese some 60-80% of the territory they claimed. MacArthur's words – *'I shall return'* - were cited as an inspiration to the resistance and became one of the most common pieces of graffiti to be seen on the islands.

THE FALL OF MALAYA

As the Japanese consolidated their beachhead at Kota Bharu on the north east coast of Malaya in early December 1941, more Japanese forces swept through Siam (now Thailand) to the north and then struck at western Malaya. Both armies then moved south as fast as they could, overwhelming all resistance and sending Commonwealth troops,

MAIN IMAGE: Philippines Landing, Japanese troops street fighting on Mindanao

settlers and natives alike fleeing desperately before them. Many of the Japanese soldiers had been equipped with bicycles which speeded up their advance and they were supported by highly mobile light tanks which were far better than anything the Commonwealth forces could put in the field. It was a complete shock to the Allies who had previously been told that the Japanese were poor fighters and no match for Empire men. Of the 65,000 troops Japan committed to the offensive, most were battle hardened from the brutal war in China. The Empire men had mostly never fired a shot in anger before.

Within days, Japan had air superiority too, and with the destruction of Task Force Z, there was no naval opposition to further landings of reinforcements, equipment and supplies in support of actions all along the east coast. In a desperate attempt to slow them down, Royal Engineers demolished over 100 bridges on the roads south, but the Japanese sapper units proved particularly efficient in repairing them and keeping the advance moving. Such was the speed of the Allied retreat that many of their wounded had to be left behind. They were routinely murdered by the advancing Japanese, shot, bayoneted or in some cases simply doused with petrol and set alight.

By the start of 1942, the Japanese effectively controlled all of Northern Malaya. Kuala Lumpur fell, undefended, on January 11 and the Japanese simply marched in. A week later, the Japanese were threatening the southern state of Johore but their advance stalled as they came up against the Australian 8th Division defending a strategically important bridge. The Japanese took 600 casualties trying

to seize the bridge before it was blown up, forcing them to divert to the west and buying the Commonwealth defenders critical time. Heading west, they encountered the poorly prepared 45th Indian Brigade – and slaughtered it.

As the Japanese punched their way south again, surviving Indian troops met up with Australian soldiers and fought a bitter four day retreat before the remnants reached the Parit Sulong bridge and were given the desperate order, *'every man for himself.'* Those who could fled, disappearing into the jungles – but the wounded had to be left behind at the mercy of the Japanese. They found none. One hundred and thirty three helpless men were tortured and then murdered. Only two survived.

On January 27, Allied troops began to retreat to the island of Singapore, abandoning the mainland altogether. Engineers then blew up the causeway connecting the island with the mainland and prepared for the siege to follow. Behind them, over 50,000 Commonwealth soldiers lay dead or were prisoners of the utterly victorious Japanese.

THE DUTCH EAST INDIES

To the Japanese, the Dutch East Indies (now Indonesia) were one of the greatest prizes to be had in the Pacific. They were rich in resources, including most especially food, rubber and oil – and poorly defended by troops more used to dealing with revolting natives than a modern

ABOVE LEFT: Newly-arrived Indian troops parade on the quayside at Singapore ABOVE MIDDLE: Royal Engineers prepare to blow up a bridge in Malaya during the British retreat to Singapore ABOVE RIGHT: Vickers machine-gun of the 1st Manchester Regiment, Malaya. RIGHT: Japanese Imperial Army military engineers hold a temporary bridge for soldiers to cross a river while marching toward Singapore

disciplined army.

The invasion began on December 17 1941. Borneo and Celebes were taken first and then Ambon, Bali, South Sumatra and Timor all fell rapidly. Colonial Dutch troops proved inadequate to the task of holding the Japanese invaders and fell back instead on a scorched earth policy, destroying valuable oil wells, airfields and critical infrastructure as they went. The Indonesians largely stayed out of it and watched.

BURMA – 'THE FORGOTTEN WAR'

The Japanese weren't particularly interested in Burma (now Myanmar). To them it was one vast disease and snake infested jungle populated by a deeply racially inferior people. It did have some relatively small oil fields and could provide rice for the growing population back on the Home Islands, but there were better sources elsewhere. It was therefore almost with reluctance that the Japanese committed resources to invading the nation in mid-January 1942, pouring across the border from Siam and heading for the capital Rangoon. They had eventually decided that they needed to protect the flank of their invasion forces in Malaya and to cut **'The Burma Road'** – the supply route from Burma that was being used to help the enemy in China. They also

resented the rule of a large Asian land by Britain and had a vague interest in the growing resistance to British rule in neighbouring India. Perhaps the vast Indian subcontinent might one day be a part of an Asia free of white rule but under Japanese domination instead…

The British it has to be said also defended Burma with a degree of reluctance. What meagre resources the British armed forces had were being prioritised for use in the Middle East, and so colonial forces were given poor training and low priority when it came to weaponry and aircraft. Japanese air power outnumbered the RAF by five to one. Those Allied soldiers in Burma would soon begin to think of themselves as **'The Forgotten Army'**.

Rangoon was captured by early March, but the British had successfully destroyed most resources of any value in the capital, including the port facilities, and much of the city was burning as the Japanese moved in. British and Empire forces then fought a long retreat north up the Irrawaddy River, pursuing a **'Scorched Earth'** policy as they went. They were joined by elements of the Chinese Army and by tens of thousands of fleeing Indian immigrants, who were hated by the native Burmese. The retreat finally ended in May 1942, with Empire forces now pushed back to Imphal in India and resorting to living rough and finding what shelter they could from the driving monsoon rains. The Japanese waited.

ABOVE LEFT: Jiang Jieshi and General Stilwell at Maymyo, April 1942 **ABOVE MIDDLE:** Troops of the 38th division fording the river at Taipah Ga, 1942 **ABOVE RIGHT:** General Stilwell discussing distribution of loads among bearers with Paul Jones during the walkout in 1942 **LEFT:** Burma natives, gathered by the roadside in the town of Maltaban, in Burma, to watch the invading Japanese march through on their way to Rangoon

THE BATTLE OF THE JAVA SEA

On January 27, a hastily cobbled together Allied fleet under Admiral Doorman attempted to stop a Japanese troop convoy in the waters north of Java. His fleet consisted of elements of the U.S. Asiatic Fleet in the region, Royal Navy vessels, Australian warships as well as Dutch vessels. The rag-tag navy included two heavy cruisers, three light cruisers, nine destroyers and a considerable number of American and Dutch submarines. The Japanese convoy was protected by two particularly powerful heavy cruisers, two light cruisers and fourteen destroyers. For seven hours, the Allied warships battled to break through the defensive cordon and get at the troop ships, but were successfully repulsed with heavy losses. After darkness, the opposing fleets clashed again and Admiral Doorman himself died when his light cruiser HNLMS De Ruyter went down. Overall, the battle resulted in a rout for the Allied ships and over 1,000 Allied sailors died. The surviving ships fled or were scattered.

THE FALL OF THE DUTCH EAST INDIES

January 28 saw Japanese invasion forces make a successful landing on Java. Combining heavy ground forces with air superiority, they drove the Dutch defenders back and back. By March 9 they had surrendered and 42,000 defenders were taken into captivity on the island. 845 Japanese soldiers were killed in the taking of the Dutch East Indies, along with a similar number of Dutch soldiers and over 1,000 Allied naval personnel. Before the Japanese occupation was over, hundreds of thousands of Indonesians would also die at the hands of the Japanese, despite enthusiastic collaboration from the Indonesian ruling classes. Many would die from forced labour or in Japanese army brothels. Others would simply starve when the Japanese exported crops from the islands for the benefit of other military units or the people of Japan.

THE FALL OF SINGAPORE

A five day bombardment of Singapore by artillery and from the air began on February 3 1942. The Japanese High Command billeted themselves in the Sultan of Jahore's palace and began to draw up invasion plans. Over on the island, the Allies knew where the Japanese commanders were but had been refused permission to strike them in case they damaged the palace. The Sultan was a good friend of the British.

The two forces squared up. The island had a number of big coastal guns at its disposal, but these were equipped with armour piercing shells intended to destroy battleships rather than ground troops. The Japanese mustered an invasion force of some 30,000 men. They were greatly outnumbered by the defenders – 85,000 Commonwealth troops had retreated to the island – but many were exhausted from the last two months of fighting and had lost much of their equipment in what was at times a near headlong rout.

Through a series of feints and dummy manoeuvres, the Japanese succeeded in fooling the Allies into believing they would attack in the north east rather than the north west. They landed instead at a particularly weak point in the Allies' defences, and 3,000 Australians found themselves fighting desperately to stave off a night landing by 13,000 Japanese. By morning, that number had swelled to 23,000. The Australians were forced back by the sheer weight of numbers. Even now, the Commonwealth High Command believed that this attack was just a decoy and that the real Japanese strike would occur to the east – and so they failed to send reserves to support the beleaguered Australians. Nevertheless the Australians continued their dogged resistance, blasting the oncoming Japanese with mortars and machine guns. They poured oil reserves into the water and set it alight, catching troops still wading ashore in a lethal sea of flames. It was valiant, but the Japanese forces were just too strong to be contained. By February 10, the Allies had fallen back to another line of defence but that quickly collapsed as Allied command became increasingly disjointed and communications started to fail.

That same day, British Prime Minister Winston Churchill blasted off a cable to his commanders, pointing out that Allied troops greatly outnumbered the invading Japanese. His frustration at their failure was obvious and he gave instructions to fight ' *to the bitter end... Commanders and senior officers should die with their troops. The honour of the British Empire and of the British Army is at stake.* '

By February 12, the Allies were desperately forming a perimeter around the city itself, which lay on the east side of the island and was by now under almost constant air attack. Inside the city, crouching in the rubble, were huddled almost one million people. From the harbor,

ABOVE LEFT: Nederlands light cruiser De Ruyter **ABOVE MIDDLE:** Japanese heavy cruiser Haguro **ABOVE RIGHT:** Men of the Malay Regiment, recruited from local native volunteers, at bayonet practice on Singapore Island **OPPOSITE PAGE; FAR LEFT:** Admiral Karel Doorman

every merchant ship that could put to sea was hauling anchor and getting out, each crammed with refugees. The Japanese increased their pressure on this perimeter and started to make significant progress.

On St Valentine's Day, 1942, the Japanese punched their way through to the Alexandra Barracks Hospital where wounded soldiers were being treated. A doctor attempted to negotiate a surrender under a white flag of truce but was swiftly bayoneted. Fifty wounded men were then murdered – some while actually undergoing surgery – as well as a number of doctors and nurses. Two hundred survivors were then kept overnight before being bayoneted to death early the next morning. A pitiful few survived by pretending to be dead.

The following day, the Allies defending Singapore found themselves almost completely out of ammunition and desperately short of food and water. They had no idea their opponents were in almost exactly the same predicament, and decided to surrender. The Japanese took their formal surrender that same evening.

5,000 Allied troops were either killed or wounded during the defence of Singapore, the majority of them Australian. The Japanese suffered very similar casualties. Untold numbers of prisoners were taken by the Japanese. Many were destined to be packed into **'Hell Ships'** and transported to work as slaves for the Japanese, on projects such as the infamous **'Burma Death Railway'**. Over one third of them would not survive their ordeal. The civilian population of the island that was ethnically Chinese fared even worse. Up to 50,000 were killed, for no other reason than the Japanese despised the Chinese. Winston Churchill would later call it the **'worst disaster'** in British military history.

During the occupation that followed, some 50,000 ethnic Chinese living on Singapore or in Malaya were systematically rounded up by the Japanese secret police, the Kempeitai, taken out to remote locations and murdered.

ABOVE: The Fall of Singapore. Some of the 120,000 British, Australian, Indian and Chinese forces captured by the Japanese forces, stand with their hands up, with Japanese guards their bayonets fixed

The Bloody Limits of Ambition

BLOCK AND RAID

Admiral Ernest J King, the head of the U.S. Fleet, threw away all America's pre-existing plans for war in the Pacific in early 1942 and came up with his own. The first part of his new strategy was to put pressure on Japan in as many places as possible to strain their limited resources. The second was a tactic called **'Block and Raid'**. Island air bases would be built to the east of Australia, defending its flank, while fast carrier forces would provide both a forward line of defence and a roaming surprise raider force, suddenly turning up to strike at Japanese bases seemingly anywhere. To defend themselves against such random attacks, he reasoned that the Japanese would have to commit heavy resources to every base they had. It was a spirited way to hold the line and inject some offensive into what until now had been a largely defensive war. The plan went into action almost immediately, with carrier-based air raids on the Gilbert and Marshall Islands on February 1, occupied Wake Island on February 24 and Marcus Island on March 4.

THE ASSAULT ON NEW GUINEA

New Guinea and the islands surrounding it had little to offer in terms of resources. It was rich only in jungle, unpleasant wildlife, stinking swamps and exotic diseases. However, the Japanese had rapidly come to realise that the Allied powers would wage any assaults on their new possessions from Australia and sought to occupy New Guinea and its Islands as a buffer in communications between the continent and the other friendly forces. The assault on New Guinea began in January 1942 when the Japanese seized the port of Rabaul on the neighbouring New Britain Island. Although the port had exceptionally useful resources, the real aim of the Japanese was to use it as a staging post for an invasion of New Guinea and then to seize the capital, Port Moresby. With Port Moresby in their grip, the Japanese could then apply considerable pressure to Australia to the south, and possibly even use it as a staging post for any future invasion of the continent.

Initial invasion plans were considerably disrupted by the arrival of a surprise U.S. carrier task force on February 20 looking to dislodge the Japanese from Rabaul on one of Admiral King's **'Block and Raid'** sorties. The Japanese detected the raiders and sent 17 Betty bombers against the ships. They lost all but two of them in the ensuing action, as

ABOVE: Imperial Japanese garrison civil affairs division members cast lines at a pond circa June 1942 in New Ireland Island, Papua New Guinea

LEFT: Fleet Admiral Ernest J King

BUT if you continue to resist ....

Then, under the beautiful tropical moon, only DEATH awaits you.

Bullet-holes in your guts---agonizing death!

You have the two alternatives.

Take your choice.

That unforgettable embrace under the beautiful moon with the warmth of HER shapely body nestled against yours; that blood-tingling kiss; that over-powering sense of passion that sweeps over you---these and many other pleasant memories you'll be able to relive again if you'll throw down your arms, surrender and prepare to get out of this hell-hole.

Grumman Wildcat fighters from the carrier Lexington rose to meet them. As the element of surprise had been lost, the carrier group withdrew but the damage to the local Japanese bomber force was considered so severe by the Japanese command that they postponed their strike on New Guinea, earning its defenders valuable extra time to prepare for the onslaught.

ASSAULT ON AUSTRALIA

Japan never quite made up its mind as to whether it wanted to invade Australia. The Kaigun were in favour and the IJA against. The Army won the day. However, the North coast of the continent was too close to the prized Dutch East Indies for comfort and still needed to be subdued.

The bombing of targets in Northern Australia started on February 19 1942, when almost 200 Japanese warplanes hit Darwin after being launched from a carrier task force in what became known as *'Australia's Pearl Harbor'*. Indeed, the four carriers involved had all participated in the original Pearl Harbor strike. The Australians had been anticipating an air raid (or worse) against Darwin and by Christmas 1941 had successfully evacuated all the white women and children from the city. The aborigines had not been evacuated.

When they came in, the raiders went for the port. As they approached, they were mistaken for American aircraft and the gunners manning the air defences hesitated. As a result, eight ships – including an American destroyer - were swiftly sunk at their moorings. Attempts to rescue survivors were hampered by 75,000 tonnes of oil being discharged into the harbor by a stricken and listing tanker. The oil swiftly caught fire. A follow up raid by over 50 bombers from Ambon an hour later hit the city and its two airfields, destroying 20 RAAF aircraft on the ground. Five aircraft were shot down by the ships at anchor and Darwin's ack-ack guns. 250 people died on the ground, mostly in the port area, but casualty figures were deliberately underestimated so as not to affect Australian moral.

In all, Japan would launch just under one hundred air raids against Australia between February 1942 and November 1943, concentrating on shipping in the coastal waters, ports, airfields, railway lines and fuel storage facilities in the main. Sixty three of those raids were directed against Darwin.

ABOVE: Australia: With the Japanese ensconced in bases on New Guinea, only a scant 400 miles from the Australian mainland, the continent 'down under' is making feverish preparations for the struggle that is to come LEFT: Propaganda leaflet dropped in Australia by The Japanese army

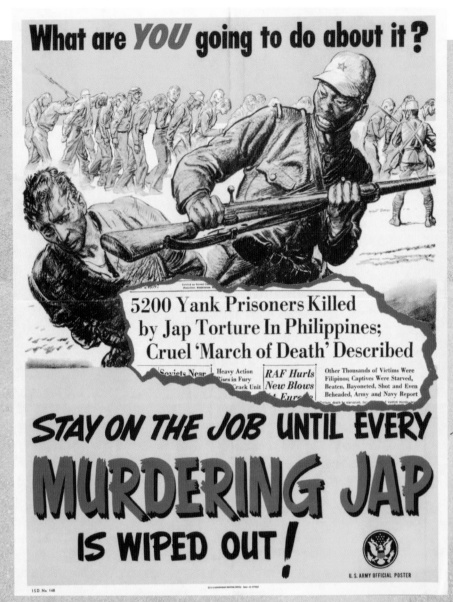

THE BATAAN DEATH MARCH

While the fighting was still going on in Corregidor in April 1942, the Japanese decided to move the Allied troops they had taken prisoner to Balanga, the capital of Bataan. As many as 80,000 Filipinos and American troops were forced to march sixty miles to their intended destination and were mistreated every step of the way. Before the march even started there were atrocities committed, especially against Filipinos whom the Japanese considered deeply racially inferior. 300-400 NCOs and men were simply murdered in just one such event. While marching through the blistering heat, the prisoners were given no food or water. They were also beaten and - if they fell behind from sunstroke, exhaustion or their wounds - they were run over by Japanese lorries, shot or bayoneted as they lay on the side of the road. Others were beheaded by Japanese officers with their ceremonial swords. In desperation, some of the prisoners took to drinking the filthy muddy water pooled on the side of the road and rapidly caught dysentery. It's estimated that anywhere between 2,500 and 10,000 Filipino soldiers died on the Bataan Death March, as it became known, along with several hundred Americans. Even when they reached their destination, the exhaustion, neglect, malnutrition and disease continued to claim victims amongst the prisoners at the rate of several hundred every day, until the final death toll reached 2,330 American men and perhaps as many as 20,000 Filipinos.

ABOVE: American prisoners using improvised litters to carry those of their comrades who, from the lack of food or water on the march from Bataan, fell along the road. Philippines **OPPOSITE PAGE; BOTTOM LEFT:** On the Bataan Death March **BOTTOM MIDDLE:** A brief rest from the Death March **BOTTOM RIGHT:** Victims of the Death March **BOTTOM LEFT:** US propaganda poster

STRIKING BACK
THE DOOLITTLE RAID

On April 18 1942, Japanese Prime Minister Tojo was deeply engaged in his paperwork whilst flying between appointments. The plane suddenly jolted violently. Peering out from his window seat, Tojo could clearly see another plane flying alongside – a bomber by the size of it. He glared angrily at the pilots for endangering his aircraft – and to his shock realised they were white and staring back at him. He barely had time to register the bomber's colour scheme or markings before it moved away – but he was in no doubt about what he had just seen. That was an American bomber – and it was heading for Tokyo.

Just two weeks after Pearl Harbor, President Roosevelt rounded up his Joint Chiefs of Staff and demanded that the Japanese Home Islands be bombed *'as soon as possible'*. It was, he said, crucial for the morale of the American People. It was also vital to shake and shock the Japanese population, who had been told they were completely invulnerable to attack.

It was obvious that, if the Americans were to mount any sort of attack on Japan, it would have to come from one of their aircraft carriers, so that was the starting point. Early in January 1942, Admiral King got an interesting suggestion from one of his captains. That captain had been watching B-25 Mitchell medium bombers taking off and landing on bases – and thought that they might, just might, be able to take off from an aircraft carrier too. The task was then turned over to a celebrated test pilot and engineer Lieutenant Colonel James Harold **'Jimmy'** Doolittle – an Army Air Force man.

Doolittle had some of the Mitchell's guns stripped away to save weight and instead installed a new fuel tank which almost doubled the bomber's capacity. His pilots would need every drop of fuel. They would have to fly to the very limit of their endurance, strike their target and then run like hell for the relative safety of Free China. There would be no possibility whatsoever of them being able to fly all the way back to the safety of their carrier – even if they could land safely, which was seen as next to impossible. The pilots and crews – all volunteers – did not know this. They were just asked to volunteer for a *'dangerous secret mission'*. They wouldn't be told any more until they set sail.

On April 1, sixteen specially modified B-25s were stowed away on board the aircraft carrier USS Hornet. They sailed the next day to rendezvous with Task Force 16 comprising cruisers, destroyers and another carrier, USS Enterprise which would provide air cover. While still 650 nautical miles from Japan, the task force was spotted by a line of Japanese picket boats. One managed to radio out a warning before it was sunk. Doolittle and the captain of Hornet realised that the element of surprise was now severely compromised and that Japanese submarines and who knows what else might be swiftly vectored onto them. They decided it was now or never. The mission was a go – even though they were ten hours ahead of schedule and 170 nautical miles from the launch point.

All sixteen B-25s made it off the carrier safely in the early light of April 18, even though none of the pilots had ever tried it before. They headed in for Japan at wave top height. Their main target was Tokyo, but some aircraft were assigned targets in Yokohama, Yokosuka, Nagoya, Kobe and Osaka. After six hours of wave-skimming, they rolled over land at

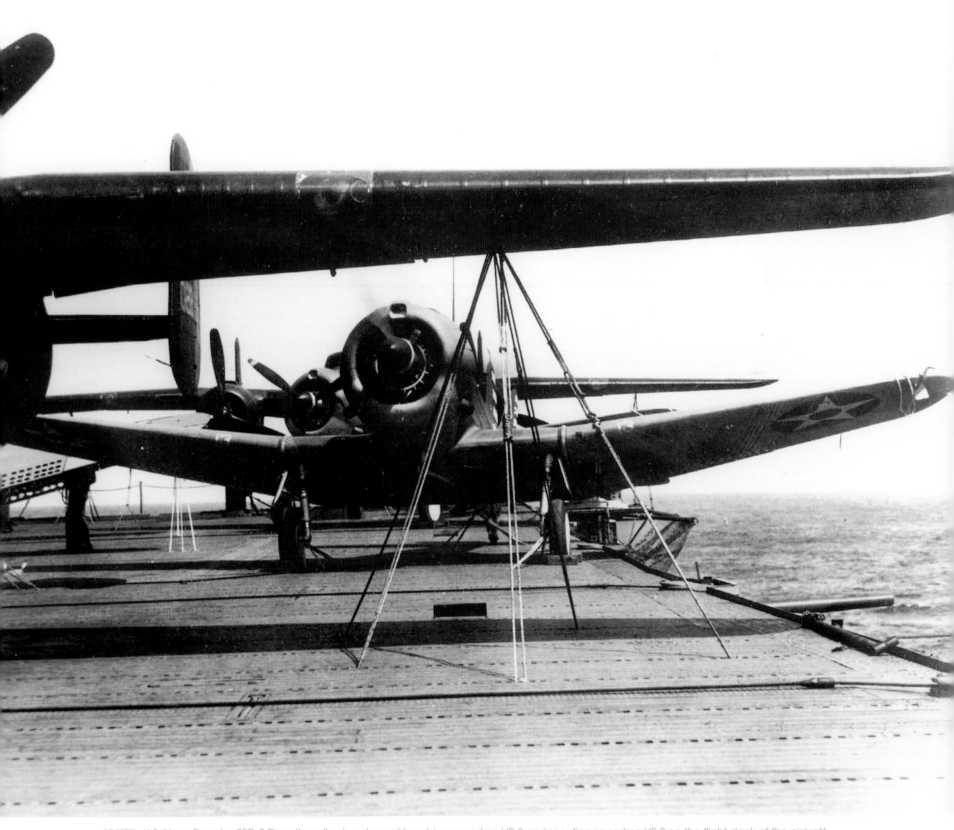

ABOVE: U.S. Navy Douglas SBD-3 Dauntless dive bombers of bombing squadron VB-8 and scouting squadron VS-8 on the flight deck of the aircraft carrier USS Hornet **OPPOSITE PAGE; BOTTOM LEFT:** Lieutenant Colonel James H. Doolittle, leader of the raiding force, wires a Japanese medal to a 500-pound bomb **BOTTOM MIDDLE:** U.S. Navy Grumman F4F-4 Wildcat fighters from Fighting Squadron VF-6 pictured on one of the aircraft elevators on board the aircraft carrier USS Enterprise **BOTTOM RIGHT:** American Entertainer Red Skelton with "Doolittle Dood It" newspaper headline

last. As they flew at rooftop height, Japanese civilians in the streets waved at them and cheered. They had no idea they were American bombers. The fliers encountered some light anti-aircraft fighter and drew the attention of a few Japanese fighters up on patrol, but no B-25s were lost in the approach. The guns of B-25 Whirling Dervish did account for one Zero, while the B-25 Hari Kari-er claimed two Zeros downed. When they weren't fending off Zeros, the gunners strafed any military targets they could see just below them.

By the time they reached their targets they had gently climbed to 2,000 feet. In Tokyo, the majority of bombs hit an oil tank storage facility, a steel mill, factories and several power plants. Elsewhere, the new Japanese light aircraft carrier Ryuho was hit, putting her out of action for seven months.

Bombs gone, fifteen of the B-25s raced for China. As they approached the Chinese coastline, they were desperately short of fuel because of their premature launch. Night was falling and weather conditions were worsening fast. They would never make the Chinese fields prepared to receive them. Instead the crews now took the decision to either bail out or crash-land their aircraft. One crewman was killed after parachuting out. (It was discovered later that he had landed safely, but then accidentally walked off a cliff while trying to gain his bearings). Two more drowned as their plane crash-landed in the shallows. Doolittle himself landed in a huge heap of dung. He thought it particularly apt, because he had just lost all of his aircraft and he thought his superiors would roast him for it if he ever made it back. He expected a court martial. Instead he would receive the Medal of Honor and promotion. The sixteenth B-25, cut off from the rest, made it to Russia, where the plane and crew were seized.

Eighty men went out on what became known as the Doolittle Raid. Of those, three died on the night their planes were abandoned. Eight were captured by the Japanese and of those three were murdered and a fourth died of maltreatment. Five were interred by Russia until they escaped with the connivance of Russian intelligence agents the following year. The rest made it home, an incredible feat made possible by the famous American missionary John Birch and untold numbers of Chinese who risked everything to help them. Many suffered horrific fates in the Japanese reprisals which followed. In their fury, according to the Smithsonian, the Japanese laid waste to 20,000 square miles of China.

2,000 more victims died in the city of Yushan alone and after that was done, elements of the secret bacteriological warfare group, Unit 731, moved in to conduct horrific biological warfare experiments on the local population. Being incompetent as well as evil, they managed to give 10,000 of their own soldiers the plague.

The Doolittle Raid was never expected to achieve much in the way of serious damage to Japan – and it didn't – but it did shake every person in Japan from the Emperor to the lowest peasant. They tried to shrug it off, referring to it in English language propaganda as **'The Donothing Raid'** – but the truth stung. America was elated when it heard the news. Morale soared. And there was one last, totally unplanned for consequence. Rattled by the raid, Admiral Yamamoto became convinced that to secure the Home Islands it was essential to seize the island of Midway.

And at Midway, everything would change.

THE BATTLE OF THE CORAL SEA

The new Japanese landings on New Guinea and Tulagi were Codenamed Operation Mo. Troop ships would be supported by three aircraft carriers and supporting warships as they left Rabaul for their designated targets – Tulagi and Port Moresby. However, American intelligence intercepted Japanese signals and, having already broken their codes, despatched two U.S. Navy carrier task forces and a joint Australian-American cruiser force to intercept them. The scene was set for the first big carrier showdown of the war.

The first clue the Japanese had that American carriers were in the area was when they invaded Tulagi on May 3-4 1942. Although the troops got ashore safely, several of their naval escorts including a destroyer and three minesweepers were sunk by U.S. Navy aircraft off the carrier Yorktown. The Japanese responded with great excitement. Their carriers would sweep out of the Solomon Seas and hunt down and destroy the American carriers. That would constitute a great victory. The land invasions were set aside.

The opposing carrier fleets first sighted and attacked each other on May 7, sending waves of aircraft against each other. On the first

RIGHT: Survivors of the sinking of the US aircraft carrier Lexington climb aboard another ship following the battle of the Coral Sea

TOP RIGHT CORNER: Track chart from Japanese sources showing the movement of carrier Shoho and accompanying forces during the Battle of the Coral Sea, April-May, 1942

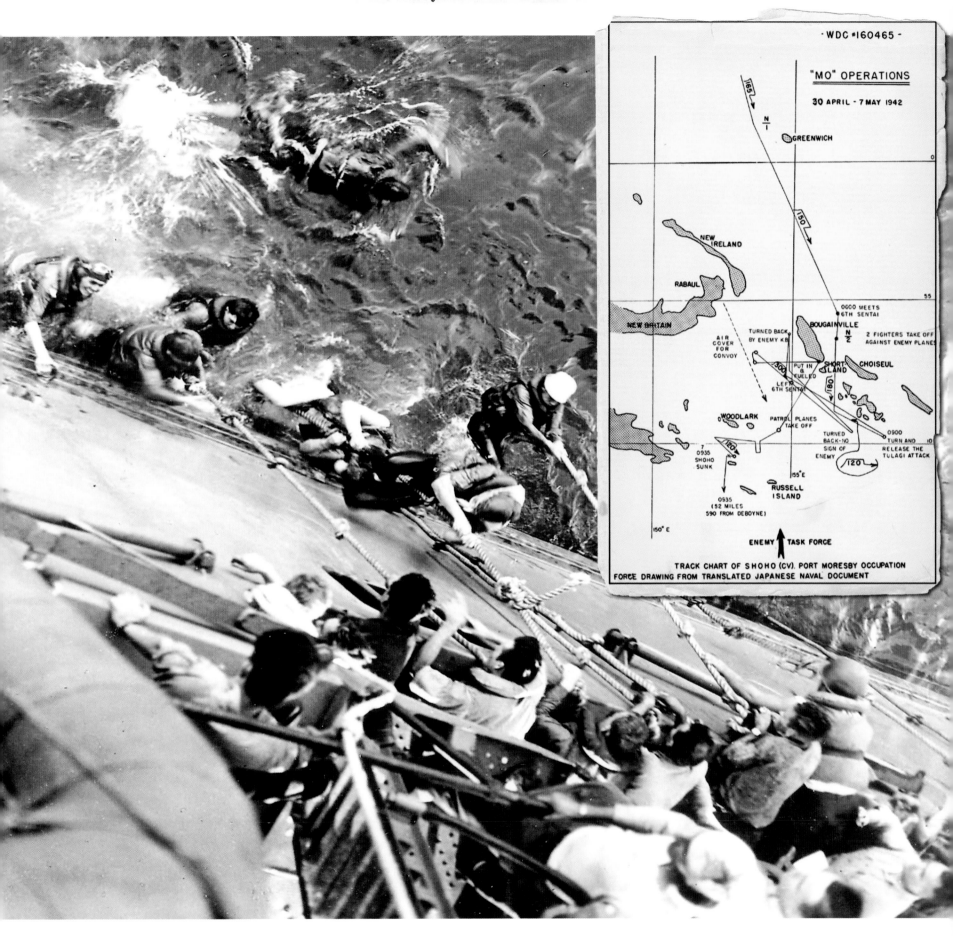

WDC #160465

"MO" OPERATIONS

30 APRIL - 7 MAY 1942

TRACK CHART OF SHOHO (CV). PORT MORESBY OCCUPATION
FORCE DRAWING FROM TRANSLATED JAPANESE NAVAL DOCUMENT

day, the light carrier Shoho was sunk in just a matter of minutes after being attacked with bombs and torpedoes by aircraft off the Lexington and Yorktown, while the Americans lost a destroyer, the USS Sims to air attack. Only 14 of her crew survived. As darkness fell, in all the confusion one Japanese flight got lost and accidentally attempted to land on an American carrier before realising their mistake and racing off again with ack-ack shells bursting all around them.

The next day, American airmen from the Yorktown succeeded in seriously damaging a second carrier, the Shokaku. All the torpedoes launched against the carriers missed but bombs created havoc on its forecastle and tore up its hangars and flight deck. Further strikes from a later wave of dive bombers off the Lexington added to the damage. The carrier then limped away from the battle under destroyer escort. In return Japanese aircraft damaged the Yorktown and so seriously blitzed the Lexington with first torpedoes and then bombs that it had to be scuttled.

Each having suffered heavy and stinging losses, both sides withdrew. The Japanese High Command were also forced to cancel their troop landings until the summer of 1942. It was the first time in the war that a major Japanese offensive had been halted in its tracks and the damage to the Japanese carriers in particular would have an unforeseen effect on the outcome of the Battle of Midway the following month.

ABOVE LEFT: USS Yorktown ABOVE MIDDLE: Japanese light carrier Shoho under attack by U.S. Navy planes during The Battle of the Coral Sea ABOVE RIGHT: Imperial Japanese Navy aircraft carrier Shokaku's fighter squadron RIGHT: Australian and Dutch prisoners of war at Tarsau in Thailand OPPOSITE PAGE: On the aircraft carrier USS Yorktown, Grumman F6F-3 fighters warm up on the flight deck

THE BURMA DEATH RAILWAY

As the war in Burma intensified, the Japanese needed a reliable way to get supplies to their forces. They decided to build a 258 mile long railway between Ban Pong in Siam and Thanbyuzayat in Burma, using POWs and Asian natives as forced labour. Such a railway had been considered before by the British Empire, but the terrain was too daunting with thick jungles and many rivers that would need bridging.

Allied prisoners were set to work on the task from May 1942. They finished ahead of schedule in October 1943. They slaved under the most inhumane conditions without any proper tools, with little food or medicine, enduring frequent beatings and at the mercy of ravenous

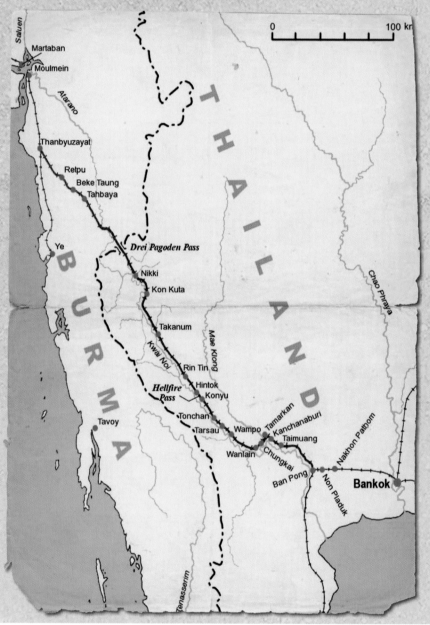

brothels. These were the so-called **'Comfort Women'**. As late as 2007, the Japanese Government was still arguing that there was *'no evidence of coercion'* and that these women were there voluntarily.

Only between 20 and 50,000 Japanese were taken prisoner by the Allies. Partly, this was due to a willingness to fight to the death but also a growing lack of enthusiasm by Allied troops to take prisoners. On many occasions, wounded or surrendered Japanese would suddenly turn on

jungle diseases. The worst conditions were reserved for the Asian native workers, many of whom had been enticed to work on the railway by adverts in newspapers. Some had even brought their wives and children with them…

Building the railway cost the lives of 6,904 Britons, 3,098 Dutch, 2,646 Australians, 131 Americans – and over 180,000 Asian slave labourers. Of the Japanese who oversaw the construction, 111 faced accusations of war crimes at the end of the conflict and 32 were sentenced to death.

The Japanese established over 500 POW and slave labour camps during World War II. 36,260 American servicemen were taken prisoner. 13,381 died in captivity. Of the 50,000 British POWs, 12,433 never returned home and 8,031 of 21,000 Australian prisoners did not survive. 25,000 of the 100,000 Dutch servicemen captured died in captivity. A further estimated 10,720 POWs died on board the **'Hell Ships'** transporting them to the camps. The cause of death of prisoners varied widely. Malnutrition, exhaustion, disease, neglect, beatings and torture counted for many. Cold blooded murder counted for others. Some were subjected to medical experiments including living vivisection, while others were simply worked to death. It should also be remembered that some 200,000 women were held captive and used as prostitutes in Japanese

ABOVE LEFT: Entrance of a comfort station. "Services of Yamato nadeshikos who devote their body and soul (to you)" "Victorious warriors of the Holy War, Very welcome!" **BOTTOM RIGHT:** Map showing the Death Railway line **FAR RIGHT:** Admiral Yamamoto Isoroku

their captors and try to kill them. A distinct lack of trust soon grew up amongst Allied soldiers. The other reason was that – despite Roosevelt's attempts to keep it secret – the appalling Japanese treatment of Allied prisoners was known to every man. In 1944, the Allies had to make special efforts to persuade their troops to take Japanese prisoners – an effort that succeeded to some extent.

THE BATTLE OF MIDWAY

'There is no choice but to force a decisive fleet encounter...
If we set out from here to do that and we go to the bottom of the
Pacific in a double suicide, things will be peaceful on the
high seas for some time'

Admiral Yamamoto

When the Japanese prepared to invade Midway in early May 1942, they had no real interest in the obscure island itself, a hunk of rock some 1200 miles north west of Hawaii. Instead, the operation was a plan to draw out the American aircraft carriers and destroy them. They called it Operation Mi.

Admiral Yamamoto was by now critically concerned about American carrier power, and the Battle of the Coral Sea just a month before had convinced him that they presented perhaps the greatest threat to Japan achieving naval dominance in the Pacific. The entire Japanese nation was also still smarting from the Doolittle Raid, launched from a carrier and which had allowed America to strike at the heart of the Home Islands and endanger the Emperor. Such a thing could not be permitted to happen again. Midway was chosen because it was sufficiently close to Pearl Harbor to attract the enemy carriers and draw them into a trap.

The trap was set, but not in the way Yamamoto had envisaged. Unknown to him, Japanese JN25 naval codes had been broken and the Americans knew almost exactly what he was up to. Most important of all, they knew where his carriers would be on a particular day and date. Carrier battles relied on one side locating the other first and getting its aircraft away to devastate the opponent's ships while the other was still searching. The Americans would have the critical advantage.

Task Force 16 set sail from Pearl Harbor on May 28, comprising the carrier Enterprise escorted by six cruisers and nine destroyers. Two days later, the carrier Yorktown sailed to join her. Despite having suffered severe battle damage during the Battle of the Coral Sea, she had been fully repaired in just three days at Pearl Harbor. Waiting for them was Yamamoto's fleet comprised of four large and two medium carriers, eleven battleships and numerous cruisers and destroyers.

On June 4, Japanese warplanes started attacking Midway Island, while the American carrier force successfully located the position of the Japanese carriers. They were attacked at first by ten torpedo bombers based on the island, but the slow lumbering machines were met with a wall of anti-aircraft fire from the Japanese and rapidly lost seven aircraft without hitting anything. Now B-17s and Vindicators from Midway bombed the carriers, but without any real results. The Japanese carriers launched Zero fighters to intercept them, again without much success.

The Zeros had returned to their carriers and were refuelling and rearming when the Japanese received the news that four squadrons of American aircraft were inbound on their position - with their fighters still trapped on the flight decks. Unknown to the Japanese, the American warplanes – comprising 67 Douglas Dauntless dive-bombers, 51 Devastator torpedo-bombers and 20 Wildcat escort fighters were suffering difficulties too. They had struggled to find the carriers and were now running critically low on fuel. A number of the fighters had already exhausted their fuel and had ditched in the sea and the bombers were critically short of fighter cover as they made

their attack run.

The Devastator torpedo bombers went in first, meeting a wall of solid anti-aircraft fire. The Japanese had managed to launch around 50 of their Zeros and these went after the slow and almost defenceless torpedo bombers too. It was a massacre. The Devastators were torn from the skies. 47 of them were lost and not a single torpedo hit the Japanese carriers. Enjoying the delicious spectacle of the massacre, the Japanese officers and crew made one fatal error: They forgot to look up. They had no idea that, above them, three squadrons of American Dauntless dive-bombers were now massing – the aircraft the Japanese fearfully referred to as **'Hell-divers'**. When they struck, it came as a complete surprise. The first bombs to fall on the carrier Akagi punched into a store of torpedoes, detonating them all and starting a raging inferno that soon reached the ship's fuel supplies. Akagi was finished. The Kaga was hit next, bombed by almost two full squadrons of dive bombers. The captain was killed when the bridge was hit and four more strikes followed in rapid succession, triggering a fire so fierce that the ship could not be saved. Three more bombs, this time from bombers off the Yorktown, hit the carrier Soryu, convincing the captain to start abandoning ship. It all happened in the space of just five minutes. In those five apocalyptic minutes, the Japanese lost three of their most important warships.

The fourth carrier, Hiryu, did manage to get forty of its aircraft off. Those warplanes then found and critically damaged the American carrier Yorktown with two successive waves, landing two torpedo strikes and three bombs on target. Its position now revealed, the

ABOVE LEFT: Japanese Destroyers Saghir, Amagiri and Asagiri **ABOVE MIDDLE:** An Imperial Japanese Navy "Zero" fighter on the carrier Akagi
ABOVE RIGHT: U.S. Navy Douglas TBD-1 Devastators unfolding their wings on the deck of USS Enterprise on the first day of the Battle of Midway
RIGHT: U.S. Navy Douglas SBD-3 "Dauntless", of USS Enterprise´s Bombing Squadron Six , is parked on board USS Yorktown. This plane, damaged during the attack on the Japanese aircraft carrier Kaga that morning, landed on Yorktown as it was low on fuel. It was later lost with the carrier

ABOVE: On board the U.S. Navy aircraft carrier USS Yorktown (CV-5) during the Battle of Midway, shortly after she was hit by three Japanese bombs on 4 June 1942 **OPPOSITE PAGE; BOTTOM LEFT:** Black smoke pours from the U.S. Navy aircraft carrier USS Yorktown (CV-5), at circa 1400 hrs on 4 June 1942 **BOTTOM MIDDLE:** The U.S. Navy aircraft carrier USS Yorktown being abandoned by her crew **BOTTOM RIGHT:** Chester Nimitz

Hiryu was found and struck by 24 American dive bombers from the Enterprise six hours later, with the result that it had to be scuttled the next day (The Yorktown stayed afloat for a while longer but was finished off by a Japanese submarine as it tried to limp back to Pearl Harbor.)

As the two sides disengaged, it quickly became obvious that the American offensive had succeeded beyond almost anyone's expectations. The Japanese had lost four carriers and – already dangerously overstretched by the war effort as they were – would never be able to adequately replace them. The Americans had lost one carrier, but the nation was rapidly discovering its own industrial might and the ship would be replaced with comparative ease. The Japanese had also lost a heavy cruiser, over 3,000 experienced men and 270 aircraft. In contrast, the Americans had lost the Yorktown, one destroyer (hit completely by accident as the Japanese went after the Yorktown), 370 men and 130 aircraft. Three American airmen were captured during the battle. After a brutal interrogation, they were weighted down and thrown overboard. Thirty-seven Japanese naval personnel were rescued by American warships. They all lived.

American Admiral Chester Nimitz dared to make a bad joke when he later announced, *'Perhaps we will be forgiven if we claim we are about midway to our objective!'* After such a resounding victory, he could be forgiven. Everything had changed in five minutes. Just six months after Pearl Harbor, the Japanese were to all intents and purposes defeated. They just didn't realise it yet.

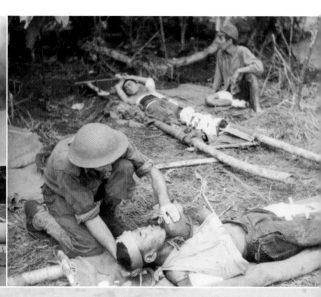

WAR IN THE ALEUTIAN ISLANDS

The Aleutian Islands off Alaska bothered the Japanese as they posed a threat to the Home Islands from the far north. Hostilities began on June 3 1942 with a carrier-based air raid against Dutch Harbor on the island of Unalaska. The raid was almost a total failure, with many Japanese aircraft lost due to atrocious weather conditions and alert American fighter aircraft. The harbor was bombed more successfully the next day. Japanese troops then invaded the islands of Kiska and Attu on June 6, and June 7 respectively.

America took two months to mount an effective response but by August 1942 was capable of launching regular bombing raids against Kiska Harbor, the major port for shipping established by the Japanese. The water around the islands became a playground for Japanese and American submarines, making them highly dangerous. On just one day the American submarine Growler managed to sink a Japanese destroyer and critically damage two more. As the war progressed, Japanese supply ships were no longer able to reach the Aleutians and the beleaguered Japanese outposts had to be resupplied solely by submarine.

NEW GUINEA –
THE ASSAULT CONTINUES

After the Japanese failed to land troops close to Port Moresby during the Battle of the Coral Sea, they decided to concentrate their strength at Milne Bay on the eastern tip of the island and at Buna, further north along the east coast, where they eventually massed over 11,000 men. The troops from Buna, who had landed on July 2 1942, then attempted to assault Port Moresby via the Kokoda Track over the rugged and forbidding Owen Stanley Mountains which separated the forces. What they had been told was a road passable by vehicles turned out to be very little more than a jungle footpath. They persevered – and kept coming, Twenty miles out from Port Moresby, Australian troops finally managed to slow the advancing Japanese with a desperate fighting retreat and then counter-attacked with fresh troops on September 26 with a brilliance that routed the Japanese forces. Thousands died in the chaotic retreat, tumbling and scrambling back down the Kokoda Trail, not only in battle but from hunger, exhaustion and disease.

The Japanese never even succeeded in gaining any significant foothold at Milne Bay. 8500 Australian soldiers and 1,300 American troops were rushed into place there. The Japanese Army took one look at the task and refused to attack. It insisted the Kaigun marines do the fighting instead. 1,250 naval infantry from the Japanese Navy then dutifully arrived on August 25 1942. It was soon clear that they had greatly underestimated the number of Allied troops in place and also the sheer supporting air power the Allies could bring to bear from newly built air fields in the region.

After struggling off the beaches, there followed two weeks of fighting. Australian troops from the 7th Division fought with a particular fury after discovering some of their own men tied to trees having been bayoneted to death. Above them, the Japanese had nailed up a sign saying, *'it*

ABOVE LEFT & MIDDLE: Burning oil tanks at Dutch Harbor ABOVE RIGHT: Japanese wounded during the Battle of Buna-Gona receive medical attention from Australian personnel OPPOSITE PAGE; TOP LEFT: USS Buchanan alongside USS Wasp to refuel, while en route to the Guadalcanal-Tulagi invasion area TOP MIDDLE: USS Enterprise supporting the first day of the Guadalcanal and Tulagi landings TOP RIGHT: U.S. Marine Corps amphibian tractors move toward Guadalcanal Island BOTTOM RIGHT: Machine gun guards Matanikao River bathers from Japanese snipers

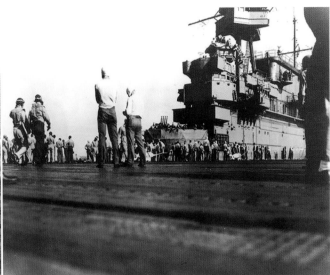

took them a long time to die'. The Japanese were progressively whittled down as a fighting force despite receiving some reinforcements and the decision was reluctantly taken to withdraw. Some left by sea under cover of a naval bombardment, others attempted to trek north to join up with forces at Buna. Around 700 Japanese soldiers were lost in the action. The Allies lost 171 men. It was the first time that Allied troops had successfully stopped the Japanese dead in their tracks in a land campaign, and it provided a solid boost to morale.

GUADALCANAL

East of New Guinea, north of Australia, the Solomon Islands were identified by the Japanese as an important strategic asset from which to block shipping routes between Australia and America. They might even prove useful if Japan ever decided to invade Australia. In May 1942, the Japanese landed advance forces to construct an airfield on the island of Guadalcanal, a 2,500 square mile, humid, stinking, jungle-covered rock. By the end of June, they had three thousand troops in place guarding it.

Understanding the potential danger, the Allies launched their first offensive of the Pacific War to retake the island and seize the airfield for themselves. On August 7 1942, the U.S. Marines came ashore on Guadalcanal 10,000 strong, while 3,000 more marines attacked the neighbouring islands of Tulagi, Gavutu and Tanambogo. Three carriers - the Saratoga, the Wasp and the Enterprise – provided air cover while

ABOVE: US Newsboard on Guadalcanal, Solomon Islands OPPOSITE PAGE; TOP LEFT: Members of the 1st Division on Guadalcanal TOP MIDDLE: Evacuating a wounded Marine near Kokumbona River TOP RIGHT: Troops from the 164th infantry rest at Guadalcanal

being protected and supported by their own 25 ship fleet. Five more American and Australian cruisers provided cover for the landing craft.

Despite this massive assemblage of sea power, the marines achieved complete tactical surprise and landed unopposed. They then forged inland towards the airstrip through dense jungle, arriving exhausted on the evening of August 8. Again they met with no opposition, as the Japanese seemed to have fled. While the marines consolidated their hold on the airstrip, out at sea, things were not going so well. Japanese bombers proved effective against Allied warships and Admiral Fletcher began to worry about the vulnerability of his carriers as well as their fuel levels. He withdrew them. As Japanese naval forces began to arrive in strength in the area, other Allied warships withdrew too, being vulnerable to Japanese air attack without the cover from their carriers.

The marines were now effectively marooned on Guadalcanal. Japanese naval units began a bombardment of their positions, while their aircraft launched from Rabaul bombed the airfield, which had now been renamed Henderson Field by the U.S.

The Japanese came to retake Guadalcanal on August 18, ploughing through the jungle towards Henderson. Their commander, Colonel Ichiki, had a particularly low opinion of marines and thought that all it would take to rout them was one mass bayonet charge out of the trees by night. He was wrong. Well-prepared machine gun nests mowed down the Japanese troops in waves as they came on.

They broke under the withering fire and fled back towards the beach, with marine reserves in hot pursuit. As they ran they were harassed, strafed and bombed by the 19 Wildcat fighters and 12 Dauntless bombers that had successfully just been landed at Henderson from the escort carrier Long Island. Facing the enemy on three sides, the Japanese made a last stand and fought to the death rather than surrender. Of the one thousand Japanese who came ashore, barely 120 survived. Colonel Ichiki committed ritual suicide.

At sea, the Allies continued to struggle with the problem of supporting Guadalcanal in hotly-contested waters. On August 31, the carrier Saratoga was torpedoed by a Japanese submarine and had to limp away for lengthy repairs.

On September 12-13, the Japanese came again. 2,000 Japanese infantry swept towards the marine defences, bayonets at the ready, but were once again cut to ribbons by machine guns. They came in three waves and each wave was stopped and driven back. By nightfall, the Japanese counted 1,200 dead or wounded. But out at sea, the American carrier Wasp was torpedoed and sunk by a pair of marauding Japanese submarines.

In Japan there was no question of just withdrawing from the Solomons. After the disgrace they had suffered on New Guinea and the disastrous naval confrontation at Midway, they could stand no further humiliation. Guadalcanal would be won, no matter what it took. Face and morale demanded it.

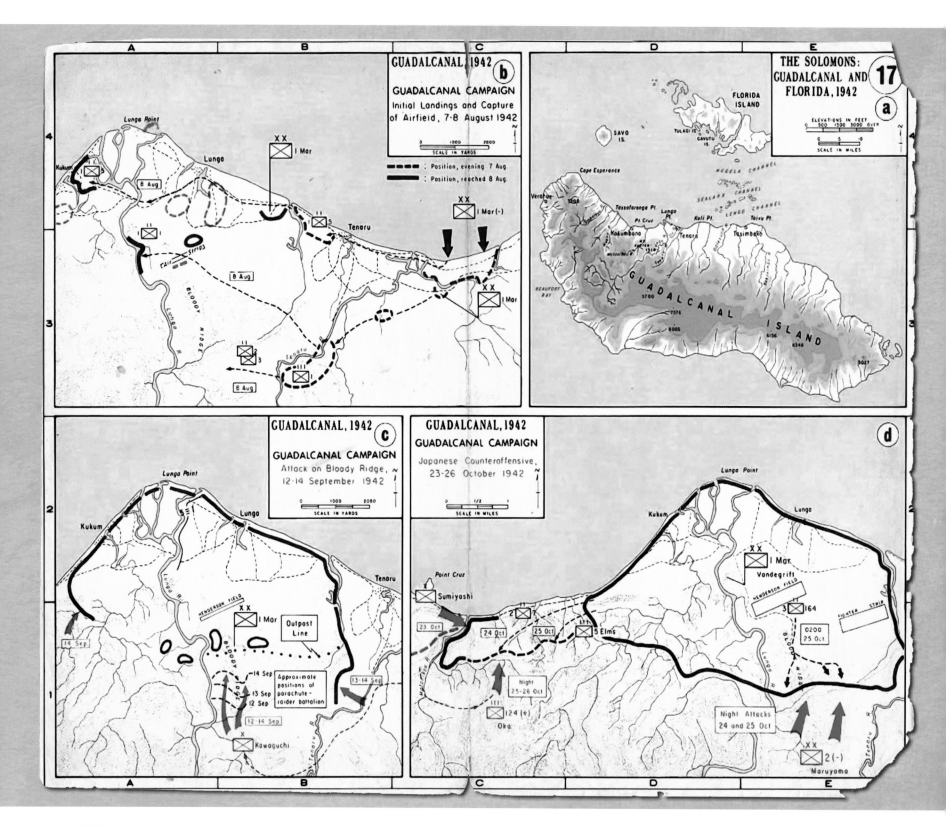

ABOVE: A series of maps showing the Guadalcanal Campaign 1942 **OPPOSITE PAGE:** Map of early operations in the battle of Buna-Gona, 16 November 1942 – 21 November 1942

THE BLOODY FIGHT FOR GUADALCANAL

In all, the Japanese threw over 31,000 men into the assault on Guadalcanal. They would lose two-thirds of them. The Americans further reinforced their Marine Corps presence to meet them and then added regular army soldiers in October. It became a grinding seven month long battle of attrition.

The Japanese came yet again on October 21. 5,600 men surged towards the American airfield only to have their attack broken up by expert artillery fire. The next day, they attacked with 7,000 men – and suffered 3,500 casualties before they retreated again. A further attack on November 4 left the Japanese with nothing but 750 casualties. The Japanese High Command's answer was to throw yet more men into the fray and launch a mass attack that would dwarf anything the defenders had seen before - but their much vaunted **'November Offensive'** was wrecked when Allied planes from Henderson caught the inbound Japanese convoy and sank six of the eleven troop transport ships.

Meanwhile, opposing carrier fleets clashed on October 26, resulting in the sinking of the Hornet and severe damage to the Enterprise. Two Japanese carriers were seriously mauled, but in particular it was the loss of experienced and virtually irreplaceable airmen and skilled flight deck crew that hurt them the most. The Japanese carriers withdrew.

By December 1942, the Japanese had finally had enough. The Emperor himself ordered a withdrawal from Guadalcanal and, over the next two months, over 11,000 surviving Japanese troops were picked up from the beaches by a naval operation which became known as the **'Tokyo Night Express'**. It's estimated that some 24,000 Japanese died on Guadalcanal. American losses were put at 1,600 – plus another 5,000 lost at sea in the fierce naval exchanges.

THE FALL OF BUNA

By November 1942, Allied forces were still working to clear the Japanese out of Buna, Gobna and Sanananda on northern New Guinea. Buna was now defended by 2,500 Japanese infantry in well prepared defensive positions. They were hit by Australian forces and elements of the U.S. 32nd Division but neither performed well in the early stage of the battle, betrayed by poor training, ill-preparedness and riven with diseases like malaria. The American forces suffered further complications after much of their supplies were lost when Japanese Zeroes sank their support convoy. The Japanese defences held and the Allies decided to effectively besiege the Japanese positions instead. Some relief supplies made it in to the Japanese but never enough and there are well-established reports that on occasions they resorted to butchering and eating the Allied prisoners they had taken. No Allied prisoners were found alive at the end of the fighting.

It was not until mid-January 1943 that the Allies succeeded in finally cracking the Japanese defences. By January 21 it was all over. The Japanese had lost in the region of 13,000 dead at Buna and other defensive points, the Allies around 2,600 of which the majority were Australians. It had been a particularly bloody and messy campaign, but the Allies had learned a valuable lesson. They had got a good close up look at the high quality defensive positions the Japanese were capable of devising – and had a taste of what they would be facing as they fought back across the Pacific.

BUNA PERIMETER
16-21 November 1942
← Allied Advance
Japanese Defenses
0   3
Miles

BURMA: THE STALEMATE

During late 1942 and much of 1943, the British were able to achieve very little against the Japanese in Burma. Britain's military resources were still being prioritised for the war in the Middle East and North Africa, and significant numbers of soldiers needed to be committed to quelling the growing civil unrest in India inspired by Indian Nationalists.

The British did launch one offensive into the coastal province of Arakan in December 1942, but were easily seen off by Japanese defensive emplacements and the arrival of reinforcements through terrain thought by the British to be impassable. Their only success was achieved with a special long range penetration unit known as the Chindits. Commanded by Brigadier Orde Wingate, an irregular warfare specialist, the 3,000 strong Chindit force slipped through the Japanese lines and then waged a ferocious jungle guerrilla war to the enemy's rear. Wingate himself described it as *'having a hand in the enemy's bowels'.* They severed important Japanese lines of communications and wrecked a railway but took heavy casualties from both the Japanese and jungle disease. Only 1/3 of the soldiers returned to their base at Imphal.

ABOVE: Japanese and Korean prisoners of war captured during the Battle of Tulagi and Gavutu-Tanambogo, Solomon Islands **LEFT:** Three Japanese soldiers lie dead on the ground, killed in fighting for Raiders' Ridge in the Battle for Guadalcanal, Solomon Islands. as the Japanese were forced to retreat

The Tide Turns

OPERATION VENGEANCE

At the beginning of April 1943, American codebreakers intercepted a Japanese message revealing Admiral Yamamoto's precise movements on April 18. He was on an inspection tour of the Solomon Islands and New Guinea to boost deflated Japanese morale and on that day would be flying out of Rabaul airfield to Balalae Airfield, on an island near Bougainville in the Solomons. They knew the precise time of the flight. They knew what sort of aircraft the admiral would be in. They even knew the composition and strength of his fighter escort. It seemed like the perfect opportunity to get some hot and hard personal revenge on the man thought of as the architect of Pearl Harbor.

There were dissenting voices: Killing Yamamoto might reveal to the Japanese that their JN25 code had been broken. There was concern too that Yamamoto might be replaced by someone more competent and more virulently anti-western. Lastly, there was the moral question: Was it right to kill one particular individual in a war? Was that, in fact, cold blooded murder? Admiral Nimitz himself weighed up the pros and cons and decided the mission should go ahead. Yamamoto was fair game. The decision to target and kill Yamamoto was still above Nimitz's pay grade and eventually went all the way to the White House. Roosevelt pondered, then gave one simple instruction: Get him.

Assigned to the task were sixteen P-38 Lightnings from the 339th Fighter Squadron. Four were designated as **'the killers'** who would go for Yamamoto's transport. The rest would engage the Zero escorts and keep them too busy to come to the rescue. They were to fly 600 miles out to the intercept, **'wave hopping'** at 50 feet all the way to avoid detection. It was to be the longest fighter intercept mission of the war and, in private, one of the commanding officers thought it was a 1,000-to-1 shot they'd ever even see Yamamoto's aircraft given the tiny margin for error that the timing allowed. He also thought it was close to a suicide mission.

The P-38s took off from Kukum Field on Guadalcanal at 07.25. At 0800 on April 18, 1943, Admiral Yamamoto's Betty transport took off from Rabaul, together with another Betty and a six Zero fighter escort. The P-38s spotted them an hour and a half later as they were preparing to land. The shout went out to *'go get them!'* and the P-38s climbed hard

LEFT: Official US army poster UP AND AT 'EM. BUILD MORE P-38'S
RIGHT: Lockheed P-38 Lightning

up towards their target. Everyone knew this had to be done fast. Below them, on Bougainville Island were 75 Japanese Zeros who could be scrambled on to them in minutes. As they climbed, they were spotted by the Zero escort who dived to meet them.

The first Betty was hit almost immediately by a P-38's nose-mounted 20mm cannon and four .50 - caliber machine guns. Its right engine began to smoke and sputter before the plane suddenly tipped over to the left and nearly collided with the fighter pursuing it before dropping towards the dense jungle on Bougainville Island below. The second Betty was desperately manoeuvring now to try and shake off the P-38s all swooping in for the kill. Its right engine was already hit and trailing white smoke. A second attack tore thick metal shards off the bomber before it plunged into the ocean. Both targets down, the P-38s swiftly disengaged from the Zeros and raced for home. One P-38 was later found to be missing, shot down by a Zero in the melee. Sweeping into Henderson Field, Captain Thomas G. Lanphier, leader of the **'killer'** flight radioed in, *'That son of a bitch will not be dictating any peace terms in the White House!'*

A rescue party found Yamamoto still strapped to his seat and clutching the hilt of his samurai sword. He had been flung clear on impact but was dead, pierced by two shells from an American fighter. As punishment for failing to protect the admiral, all six surviving Zero fighter pilots were ordered to stay on constant combat duty until they were shot down and killed by the enemy. Five of them died this way. A sixth escaped after losing a hand during a dogfight and thus becoming unfit to fly. For his service to the Emperor and Japan, Admiral Yamamoto was posthumously awarded the Order of the Chrysanthemum (1st Class).

RECAPTURING THE ALEUTIANS

The Aleutians were part of America and losing American soil to the Japanese had always stung. Operations to take back the Aleutians began on May 11 1943. American forces initially struggled to seize the island of Attu. The terrain – mostly tundra - was harsh and unforgiving, and the climate literally freezing. The Japanese did not contest the landings but instead moved to higher ground inland. Both sides struggled to fight in the ferocious conditions and more Americans died of disease on the island than were killed by Japanese action. More too fell victim to frostbite than war wounds. On May 29, the Japanese gambled everything on a huge Banzai bayonet charge. The sheer power of the attack allowed it to penetrate right through to the American rear, but in the fierce hand-to-hand combat which followed, the Japanese were wiped out almost to a man. Only 28 prisoners were taken while at least 2,350 Japanese died.

The island of Kiska was hit next, by a combined force of 34,000 Americans and Canadians. They stormed ashore on August 15 to find the island completely deserted. The Japanese garrison had successfully been evacuated in secret a fortnight earlier.

The Aleutians were now back in American hands. Plans to attack the Northernmost Japanese islands from the Aleutians were considered but never acted upon. Japan however was seriously concerned by the threat of attack from the north and felt it had to devote significant troop numbers and Kaigun resources to defend against such a possibility. The diverting of valuable resources that could otherwise be used elsewhere by the Japanese turned out to be the real benefit of the Aleutian Campaign.

ISLAND HOPPING

Japan had been stopped. The Empire had been held on its southward thrust at New Guinea and in the Solomons and its naval power had been severely compromised by major carrier engagements. Now, the Allies decided, it was time to push back. Between them, Admiral Nimitz and General MacArthur settled on a strategy called '**Island Hopping**'. Starting out mainly from their bases and territories in the south, they would blaze all-out war northwards up the occupied island chains of the Pacific, conquering one set of islands and using them as the staging post for the invasion of the next island chain to the north.

Initially, commanders thought it would be necessary to take back every island, every atoll, every rock occupied by the Japanese along the way. They soon realised however that only key targets needed to be taken and that other, less strategically important Japanese possessions could just be bypassed on the way. They would be bombed and shelled if they presented a threat, but otherwise they could simply be left to '**wither on the vine'.** Marooned in hostile seas, they would simply starve for lack of supplies and fall apart.

The Navy under Nimitz wanted to concentrate on a northbound island-hopping strategy through the Central Pacific, designed to eventually arrive to the South of the Japanese Home Islands which could

OPPOSITE PAGE: Officers and men of the Canadian Fusiliers were part of the occupation forces which moved in without meeting any resistance and took complete control of the Aleutians **ABOVE LEFT:** Soldiers unload landing craft on the beach at Massacre Bay, Attu, on 13 May 1943
ABOVE MIDDLE: Troops march up the beach at Adak Island, during pre-invasion loading for the Kiska Operation, 13 August 1943
ABOVE RIGHT: Soldiers hurling their trench mortar shells over a ridge into a Japanese position, Attu, Aleutian Island

then be either invaded or bombarded from safe Allied islands. MacArthur however also wanted a second simultaneous island hopping drive to the West to retake the Philippines as he had promised. He eventually got his way. MacArthur would lead the Western thrust while Nimitz would take his fleet and men north.

OPERATION CARTWHEEL AND THE THREAT OF RABAUL

Since the Japanese had conquered the island of New Britain in January 1942, they had turned the port of Rabaul into one of their main bases and areas of power and influence in the region. Rabaul had four significant military airstrips and was heavily defended by 110,000 troops. It also blocked the way west to the Philippines. It needed to be neutralised. Operation Cartwheel was seen as the answer to the threat.

Before Rabaul itself could be eliminated, the Allies would need to assault other Japanese territories in the region to either neutralise them or to use them as naval or air force staging posts. Operation Cartwheel began in the third week of June 1943, driving west with attacks on the islands of Woodlark and Kiriwina. Both these islands, intended to be home to new air bases, were captured unopposed. The next island target, New Georgia, proved a more daunting task to conquer. The Japanese had garrisoned over 10,000 men on the island and it took over a month (and substantial reinforcements) to crack them at the cost of over

1,000 American lives. At the end of June, the Allies had also attacked some leftover Japanese held portions of New Guinea, with a series of amphibious assaults by Australian troops that proved successful.

The Allies were now on their way to assaulting Rabaul, except that they suddenly changed their minds and decided they had no appetite for assaulting such a strong Japanese position after all. Instead, they would own the seas around it, preventing any further reinforcement or resupply and effectively laying siege to it. Emasculated, Rabaul would just be allowed to *'wither on the vine'*. While this neutralised the troops, the fighters and bombers on the island still posed a potential threat to other operations in the region. For this reason, Rabaul was hammered by Allied bombers beginning in October 1943. After a month, its ability to unleash airstrikes of any magnitude was severely diminished.

NEW GUINEA 1943

'Bugger the CO. Just give me twenty minutes and we'll have this place,'

Sergeant Tom Derrick V.C., 9th Australian Division
(just before single handedly climbing a cliff while firing his rifle and throwing grenades, wiping out ten Japanese machine gun nests at Sattleberg. Later, he said it was *'mostly my mates'*.)

ABOVE LEFT: Gunners from the Australian Army's 2/4th Field Regiment in a C-47 transport plane en-route to Nadzab in New Guinea **ABOVE MIDDLE:** U.S. Army Air Forces Douglas C-47 Skytrain transports at Nadzab airfield **ABOVE RIGHT:** Markham Valley, New Guinea. The crew of a Short 25 pounder gun from 12 Battery take up their positions on the range of the 4th Field Regiment.

As part of the 'clearance' around New Britain, Australian forces launched fresh assaults on Japanese forces still on New Guinea at the start of September 1943. The 9th Australian Division came ashore east of Lae on September 4 while the next day American paratroopers seized control of the airstrip at Nadzab. More Australian forces were then landed at the airstrip for an assault on Lae. It fell to the Allies on September 16. Australian forces then reversed and swept into the Ramu Valley to secure territory for airstrips. October 2 saw the 9th conducting fresh amphibious landings against Finschhafen where it became bogged down in heavy fighting until the end of November. By April 1944, any effective Japanese opposition still left on New Guinea had been virtually eliminated.

BOUGAINVILLE

The island of Bougainville, to the south east of New Britain, was invaded on November 1, 1943 to complete Rabaul's isolation. U.S. Marines and Army infantry came ashore at Prince Augusta Bay and were quickly threatened by Japanese warships from Rabaul. These were soon driven off by first Allied warships and then the threat posed by air power from nearby American carriers. The Allied forces stayed close to their beachhead perimeter for a couple of months, building airstrips and fending off any probing Japanese attacks while their forces at sea had some excellent successes in preventing Japanese attempts to reinforce and resupply the Japanese garrison still on the island.

It was not until March 1944 that the Japanese made one last do-or-die counterattack to drive the Americans off Bougainville. They

ABOVE LEFT: Evacuating the wounded in Bougainville **ABOVE MIDDLE:** Soldiers bury their dead in Bougainville **ABOVE RIGHT:** US Marine Corp Gunners sit ready in Bougainville **TOP:** Thomas Currie Derrick VC DCM

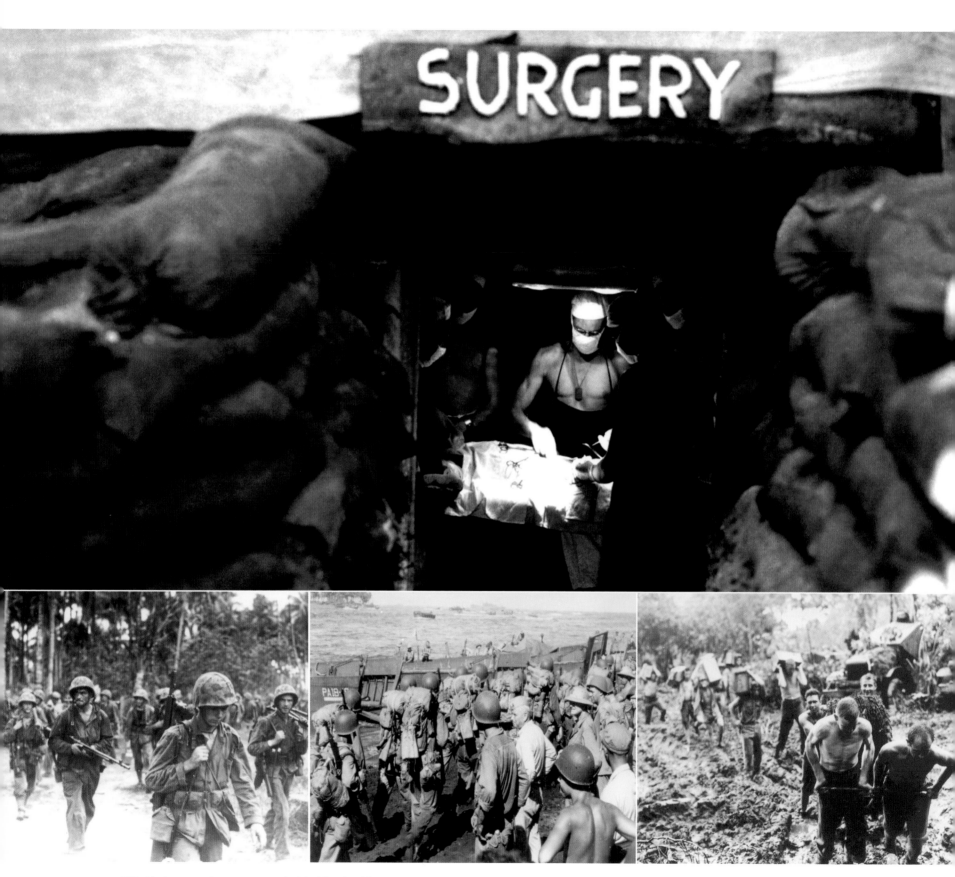

TOP: Underground surgery room, behind the front lines on Bougainville, an American Army doctor operates on a U.S. soldier wounded by a Japanese sniper **ABOVE LEFT:** Advancing Marines on Bougainville **ABOVE MIDDLE:** U.S. Marines on the beach, Bougainville **ABOVE RIGHT:** The mud on Bougainville proves heavy going

threw 15,000 men into a grand assault on the perimeter. The first wave, launched on March 9, made some inroads before being pushed back by American counterattacks and intense support fire from destroyers offshore. The second wave came on March 12 and was foiled this time by a combination of tanks and air power. Other Japanese attacks followed, but they were weak and insubstantial. They were shattered as a fighting force by Allied reinforcements the following month, and disease and hunger soon set in. The survivors foraged for snakes, rats and crocodiles to eat. When they tried to grow crops in any degree of organisation, the Allies dropped napalm on them. 8,200 Japanese soldiers were killed in combat on Bourgainville. More than double that number died from disease or starvation.

THE GILBERT ISLANDS – OPERATION GALVANIC

The Gilberts were the start of the Allies northbound 'Island Hopping' campaign. A chain of islands arranged north-south and straddling the equator to the north east of the Solomons, the islands officially belonged to the British Empire but were now occupied by the Japanese who had recently heavily reinforced them. For the Allies, their only real importance were as useful staging posts for future strikes against the Marshall and Marianas islands.

Supported by naval bombardment and carrier-based airstrikes,

marines first came ashore on the Island of Tarawa on November 20 1943. The 4,800 Japanese defenders fought with a fanatical intensity for three days, inflicting severe casualties on the marines before they were themselves utterly destroyed. Over 1,000 marines died on Tarawa and double that number were wounded in the fighting. Of the Japanese defenders, only 17 survived.

At the same time as Tarawa was being attacked, the Allies struck against the other heavily fortified island in the chain, Makin Atoll. American infantry went ashore on November 20 and subdued the Japanese garrison there within just two days. The soldiers only took 66 casualties and killed almost 400 Japanese, but the victory was soured by the torpedoing of the escort carrier USS Liscome Bay by a Japanese submarine lurking off the island. 644 men died aboard the ship as the torpedo slammed into an aircraft bomb storage area, causing a huge explosion which engulfed the entire vessel.

BURMA: ATTACK FROM THE NORTH

In October 1943, American General Joseph 'Vinegar Joe' Stilwell committed two Chinese divisions under his command referred to as X Force to an attack in North Burma. As the Chinese troops hit the Japanese front lines, he used his own American long range penetration brigade (known as Merrill's Marauders) to cause havoc behind enemy lines, working with elements of the more experienced British Chindits.

ABOVE LEFT: Lieutenant Commander Paul D. Buie, (center) briefs his pilots for an upcoming mission, during the Gilberts operation, aboard the aircraft carrier USS Lexington **ABOVE MIDDLE:** U.S. aircraft carrier USS Saratoga during the The Gilbert Islands campaign **ABOVE RIGHT:** Wreckage of a Japanese Aichi D3A Val dive bomber in the Gilbert Islands

ABOVE: U.S. Army troops pause for a look at a Japanese seaplane during the battle of Makin. The plane was under repair in the lagoon when the invasion started. The Japanese used it as a machine gun nest until American fliers took care of it **RIGHT:** Franklin D. Roosevelt, Churchill, C. Kai Sheck, and Mrs. Sheck in Cairo, Egypt for the conference

In April 1944, another Chinese force 40,000 strong attacked Japanese positions all along a 200 mile front. The offensive met with some success but was finally halted by the monsoon and massive Japanese reinforcements rushed into place in May 1944.

THE CAIRO CONFERENCE

In late November 1943, President Roosevelt met with British Prime Minister Winston Churchill and Chinese nationalist chairman Chiang Kai-Shek to discuss the future of the war against the Japanese in the Pacific. Josef Stalin stayed away as the Soviet Union was not involved in the conflict. Sitting almost literally in the shadow of the Pyramids, the three leaders declared that they were working towards the unconditional surrender of the Japanese without seeking any territorial benefits to their own nations. It was a carefully balanced declaration, mindful of the growing hostility to western empires in the region.

THE MARSHALL ISLANDS

The Marshall Islands were the next logical place for the Allies to strike after the Gilberts, lying relatively close by to the north. Kwajalein Atoll was the first target, assaulted by American infantry and marines on January 31 1944 after being pummelled in a fierce combined aerial and naval bombardment. The Japanese garrison managed to resist for barely four days, after which all but 105 of its 8,000 original defenders lay dead.

To support the operation, Truk Atoll, an important Japanese base and port to the west in the Caroline Islands, was attacked by warships and carrier-based aircraft on February 17 and 18. From Truk, Japanese planes could reach the Marshalls and disrupt Allied operations, so it had been decided to neutralise it. Three Japanese light cruisers, six destroyers, more than twenty-five merchant and troop ships were sunk and 270 Japanese aircraft accounted for, mostly still on the ground. Five days later, Eniwetok Atoll was stormed and taken.

THE JAPANESE INVASION OF INDIA – OPERATION U-GO

The Japanese finally felt confident enough to move into India at the start of 1944, using their 15th Army. They targeted the city of Imphal, a major army garrison, and the nearby town of Kohima as their main initial objectives, coming across the Chindwin River on March 8 1944. It was not anticipated to be a big fight. The Japanese would show up in strength and the British and their imperial lackeys would simply run away. So confident were the Japanese that they even had Korean **'Comfort Women'** flown in to be used in the big celebration after the inevitable victory.

They were surprised almost immediately by the level of hard resistance they encountered and the Allies' capability to move both men and supplies around by air to where they were most needed. They expected the British to retreat. Instead, they dug in and fought hard. A month later, the Japanese were still fighting to take Imphal, much to their dismay. They launched several offensives which were all fought off and the Allies proved so strong that they were even able to launch their own counterattacks. The relatively small Commonwealth forces at Kohima also managed to withstand a siege until it was relieved and the

ABOVE: A SBD-2 Dauntless dive bomber on the carrier USS Enterprise prepares for takeoff during the 1 February 1942 Marshall Islands Raid TOP RIGHT: Japanese troops performing a close combat attack on Yüeh-Han Railroad

British and their Empire compatriots were starting to go on the offensive aided by Chindit raids behind Japanese lines when the monsoon rains brought an effective end to all fighting in May.

The Japanese forces ranged against them had received heavy casualties in the fighting. Their lines of supply had proved weak and many of their soldiers were now suffering from severe malnutrition. Disease was rife in the ranks. Despite orders to fight on, they retreated and by June were streaming back in ignominious defeat across the Chindwin River. What was supposed to be the start of a glorious new advance had turned to Japan's greatest military defeat to date. Up to 60,000 Japanese soldiers had perished and another 100,000 were too sick or malnourished to continue fighting. The Allies lost 2,269 men.

OPERATION ICHI-GO

In the late spring of 1944, the Japanese somehow found half a million troops virtually from nowhere and launched their largest offensive of the Second World War in China. The aim of the offensive was to wipe out America bomber bases now situated in China in Kiangsi and Kwangsi and to firm up links between Manchuria and French Indochina on the Peking-Hankow railway. Hunan, Henan and Guangxi provinces all came under sudden Japanese occupation with many important cities lost. Although an undoubted military success, the massive operation ended up delivering few practical benefits to the Japanese. The Allies simply pulled their air bases further back out of reach and the railway supply route the Japanese had wanted was soon being regularly disrupted by Allied bombing raids.

ASSAULT ON THE MARIANAS

The Mariana Islands were considered a particular prize because, once secured, they could provide airstrips from which the new B-29 long range American bombers could reach Japan. The Japanese fully understood this too, and decided that they needed to hold the island chain at all costs to protect the Home Islands. Massive numbers of troops were positioned on the islands to prepare for the American onslaught, while a major Kaigun task force – which included five aircraft carriers and four light carriers – headed to directly confront the oncoming Allied 5th Fleet, which had seven aircraft carriers and eight light carriers at its disposal. They were heading for what the Japanese had been devoutly wishing for – the Kantai Kessen. The final battle.

THE BATTLE OF THE PHILIPPINE SEA

The rival fleets clashed on June 19 and 20 1944. The Japanese located the U.S. fleet first and flung over 400 planes against it. They were in for a shock. In pitched air battles, American fighters simply decimated their Japanese rivals in what became known as **'The Great Marianas Turkey Shoot'**, holding off carrier-based bombers and enemy raiders from the Philippines and Guam from getting anywhere near their carriers. Over 600 hundred Japanese aircraft would be shot down for the loss of 123 Allied planes over the course of just two days. The relatively new American Grumman F5F Hellcats proved themselves to be fighters of truly superior capabilities, particularly against Japanese pilots who were largely inexperienced. Most of their veterans had been killed by now. Better American shipboard radar also played a role in the slaughter.

On that first day of battle, although the American carriers could not locate the enemy, U.S. Submarines did. They torpedoed and destroyed two carriers – the Taiho and Shokaku. The Taiho had its fuel tanks ruptured and its largely inexperienced crew could not handle the damage control required, resulting in the ship falling apart bit-by-bit until the continuous igniting of isolated pockets of fumes finished the ship off. When the Shokaku was hit, its flight deck was full of planes being armed and fuelled. The exposed aviation fuel, ammunition and bombs all went up, consuming the doomed ship in a series of huge explosions in a matter of minutes. 1,263 men on board died in a sea of fire.

Both submarines escaped, although hounded by the stricken carriers' escort destroyers. The following day, American aircraft - four Grumman Avengers from Belleau Wood - sunk the carrier Hiyo with bombs and torpedoes. The Japanese fled, and their naval strength would never recover.

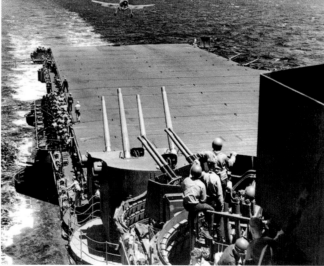

ABOVE LEFT: Fighter plane contrails in the sky over Task Force 58 aboard USS Birmingham, during the "Great Marianas Turkey Shoot" of The Battle of the Philippine Sea **ABOVE MIDDLE:** Grumman F6F-3 fighter landing aboard the USS Lexington, flagship of Task Force 58 **ABOVE RIGHT:** A Marine patrol on Saipan comes across a Japanese mother, four children and a dog, who took shelter from the fierce fighting in that area

SAIPAN — OPERATION TEARAWAY

Two days before the Battle of the Philippine Sea, a first wave of 8,000 marines had stormed ashore on Saipan – the largest of the Mariana Islands at 85 square miles and home to over 25,000 Japanese civilian immigrants - after the 30,000 strong Japanese garrison had been softened up by two days of aerial and naval bombardment. They were the first of some 71,000 troops the Allies would eventually commit to the island. There was fierce resistance from Japanese beach emplacements, which managed to inflict heavy casualties on the men coming ashore as well as knocking out 20 amphibious tanks, but by nightfall the marines had established a secure beachhead with over 20,000 troops safely ashore and dug in. Japanese counterattacks by night proved bloody and futile. Japanese attackers came again the next day, using women and children as human shields but were also driven back.

On June 16, elements of U.S. Infantry also came ashore and rapidly seized a Japanese airfield as the defenders fell back to the mountainous central region of the island. The Americans went up into the mountains after them but it was a cruel and protracted business, with the Japanese taking full advantage of the natural caves in the region. The Americans' response was to use flame throwers to winkle them out or burn them to death.

After the calamitous (for Japan) events of the Battle of the Philippine Sea, the Japanese commander on Saipan, Lieutenant General Yoshitsugu Saito, realised that his position was hopeless. He could neither hope for supplies or reinforcements by sea, nor air support. Saito then decided to go out in a blaze of glory – by organising the largest-scale banzai suicide bayonet charge in the history of World War Two. Gathered behind a red flag so large it took twelve men to carry, he assembled his 3,000 remaining able-bodied soldiers. Joining them were the walking wounded, many hobbling on crutches, armed with whatever they could find. (Japanese officers had given commands that all the Japanese wounded incapable of taking part should be shot dead in the field hospitals). Then came the Japanese civilians, who had been given pointed sticks and a personal promise from Emperor Hirohito that they would receive a favourable place in Heaven for dying in battle.

The rag-tag army swept down off the mountains at dawn on July 7, straight into the muzzles of the American machine guns. It was a slaughter but still they kept coming, almost destroying some elements of the American infantry by sheer weight of numbers. Major Edward McCarthy, the commander of the 2nd Battalion of the 105th Infantry later described the sight:

'It reminded me of one of those old cattle-stampede scenes of the movies. The camera is in a hole in the ground and you see the herd coming and they leap up and over you and are gone. Only the Japs just kept coming and coming. I didn't think they'd ever stop.'

It took fifteen hours to stem the tide of the desperate defenders, by which time 4,300 of them lay strewn about the battlefield. Back up in the high caves, Saito and his fellow senior commanders committed ritual

ABOVE LEFT: US Marines using every available means of transporting supplies to the front lines on Saipan **ABOVE MIDDLE:** The funeral of Japanese general Yoshitsugu Saitō, Saipan. **ABOVE RIGHT:** Flame Thrower in use, Saipan

suicide. There were very few Japanese survivors of Saipan. Over 30,000 died on the island, compared to under 3,000 Americans. Before the island was fully secure, more Japanese civilians killed themselves by jumping from high cliffs at the north tip of the island clutching their children in their arms. They had been told by the Japanese military that the Americans were cannibals and would roast and eat them if they allowed themselves to be caught.

Back on the Home Islands, the news of the fall of Saipan was greeted with shock and fear. Tojo and his government resigned after publicly promising that the Allies would never take the island. At the same time, the Emperor was deliberately moved away from responsibility for the course of the war to protect his divineness being challenged. The Japanese military could no longer ignore which way the winds of war were blowing.

THE RECAPTURE OF GUAM

American marines surged ashore to retake the island of Guam on July 21 1944. They were joined a few days later by regular infantry and, despite meeting fierce and determined Japanese resistance, the two forces joined up and came forward together. In response, the Japanese fell back to the heavy jungles and hills at the centre of the island, as they had on Saipan. They managed to hold out until August 10, when their commanding officer killed himself.

ABOVE: Marine keeping low on the beach at Saipan to avoid enemy fire, while making their way to their assigned positions **OPPOSITE PAGE;**
BOTTOM LEFT: Douglas SBD-5 Dauntless dive bombers from the aircraft carrier USS Lexington, fly over the invasion fleet off Saipan, on "D-Day", 15 June 1944 **BOTTOM MIDDLE & RIGHT:** The dead of Saipan

THE BATTLE FOR TINIAN

With Saipan secured, the Allies next went after the Marianas Island of Tinian, which was defended by a garrison of 9,000 Japanese packed into 40 square miles. Marines fresh from the fight on Saipan came ashore on July 24 and successfully fought off a number of Japanese counterattacks by night, forcing the defenders once more up into a remote rocky area riddled with caves. This time, they were driven out in just a couple of days after having murdered a number of Japanese civilians who refused to do their bidding. More civilians killed themselves, also as on Saipan, terrified of the American soldiers. A few Japanese soldiers ran off into the jungle and hid. The last one was found in 1953. The island was successfully taken in nine days.

FORTRESS MARIANA ISLANDS

With incredible speed and efficiency, U.S. Navy engineers known as Seabees began to convert each of the conquered islands into bomber bases. They built six massive runways on Tinian for the B-29 bombers that were to follow, as well as a garrison for 50,000 troops, while five more airfields were constructed on Guam. Two Japanese airbases on Saipan were repurposed for Allied use and two further airfields added.

THE PALAU ISLANDS

Even as the Northward 'island Hopping' campaign worked on converting the Marianas to their next staging post, the Westward driving 'Island Hopping' campaign was planning its next step. Before the Philippines could be retaken, it was decided that it would be necessary to neutralise the Japanese presence in the Palau Islands, to the east of the Philippines. The main Japanese garrison was on the island of Peleliu and by 1944 had swollen to some 11,000 men. There was also an airfield. The other island targeted was Anguar to the south west of Peleliu, where 1,400 Japanese were stationed. As the American task force charged with capturing the islands set out from Guadalcanal, what no one knew was that Japanese defensive experts had recently visited Peleliu – and had planned elaborate new defences designed to turn much of the island into one vast killing ground.

Before the marines went ashore on Peleliu on September 15 1944, the tiny island (of just six square miles) was subjected to a three day long pummelling from the big guns of four U.S. battleships and five heavy cruisers. The navy guns only ceased, to allow air strikes by bombers sweeping in off the three aircraft carriers, five light aircraft carriers, and eleven escort carriers assigned to the operation. At the end of the bombardment, the Navy claimed to have run out of targets and everyone expected a walkover. In reality, the Japanese had dug in so deep and so well that they had hardly been scratched.

LEFT: Two U.S. officers plant the American flag on Guam eight minutes after U.S. Marines and Army assault troops landed on the Central Pacific island **ABOVE LEFT:** Marines wading ashore on Tinian **ABOVE MIDDLE** A Water Buffalo, loaded with Marines, bound for beaches of Tinian Island **ABOVE RIGHT:** Marine riflemen and a bazooka team congregate their fire upon enemy snipers in the hills on Peleliu

The Japanese had only positioned a light smattering of troops on the beaches, but they were still able to devastate the landing craft and amphibious vehicles as the marines came in. A counterattack with Japanese tanks designed to sweep the marines back into the sea was only stopped by landed Allied tanks, artillery and overwhelming Allied air superiority. At the end of the day, the marines clung tenuously to their beachhead, but with 200 dead and another 900 men wounded. On the second day, marines took the airfield but suffered more heavy casualties from artillery raining down on them from the heights of Umurbrogol Mountain which – with its 500 interconnected caves and tunnels - had been designated as the Japanese strongpoint.

By September 26, the marines were still suffering from enemy fire from the caves and ridges of Umurbrogol Mountain. F4U Corsairs landed on the captured airbase to offer close air support and then went after the Japanese positions with rockets and with napalm. However, it soon became obvious that marines would have to go up and storm the complex itself. They tried, only to be repulsed with heavy losses time and again. In between assaults, Japanese snipers would target stretcher bearers to wear down the marines, or sneak through their lines at night and try to kill them in their foxholes as they slept. The Japanese position held out for two months until it was worn away by sheer grinding attrition. On November 24, the Japanese commanding officer committed ritual suicide.

The 81st Infantry were charged with taking the neighbouring island of Anguar. As on Peleliu, the defenders eventually retreated to a hilly area riddled with caves, tunnels, bunkers and pillboxes. Assaulting the fortifications proved exceptionally difficult and the defenders held out for over a month. American assaults had some success, either using flamethrowers or else bulldozers to seal up the Japanese in their caves alive. Resistance continued until October 22, with the Americans suffering more combat casualties than the Japanese.

The fight for Peleliu had taken 73 days and had resulted in horrendous Allied losses. The 1st Marine Division, which took some 6,500 casualties, was rendered combat ineffective for six months and the 81st Infantry Division had also been severely mauled with 3,300 casualties. It was estimated that the Allies had had to expend 1,500 rounds to kill each Japanese defender. Now that the full cost of the operation was clear, the Allied High Command squabbled about whether the taking of the Palau Islands had been necessary after all and whether the Japanese there could have interfered much with the retaking of the Philippines. Wiser heads looked at the new Japanese defensive tactics and realised that, in future, every island and every Atoll the Allies assaulted might be similarly defended...

ABOVE LEFT: A wounded Marine, while he waits for the stretcher-bearers to come for him, is given a refreshing drink of water from the canteen of a buddy while the Marines fight the enemy in the rough country of Peleliu **ABOVE MIDDLE** Peleliu airfield **ABOVE RIGHT:** Japanese plane shot down as it attempted to attack USS Kitkun Bay near Mariana Islands **RIGHT:** Sailors dressed in outlandish costumes for Crossing the Equator ceremonies en route to attack the Palau Islands

The Forging of Victory

RETURN TO THE PHILIPPINES

By mid-1944, it became obvious to the Japanese that the Americans were coming to eject them from the Philippines. Operation Cartwheel had brought the Allies a series of victories in New Guinea, the Admiralty Islands and now the island of Morotai in the Dutch East Indies. From Morotai, American bombers could strike at the Southern Philippines. They were joined by raiders from U.S. carriers.

On October 20 1944, U.S. Infantry made their first landing on the occupied Philippines, coming ashore on the island of Leyte. MacArthur himself joined them six hours later. On October 22, he would broadcast on radio, *'People of the Philippines: I have returned…Rally to me!'*

The Japanese responded in spectacular fashion.

KAMIKAZE

The notion of personal sacrifice for the good of the Emperor and Japan was well embedded in the Japanese Bushido warrior code. As long ago as Pearl Harbor, there had been serious discussion of ramming American battleships with aircraft should they prove to have anti-torpedo nets. (They didn't). In June 1944, as the Japanese position became ever-more desperate, the suggestion of organised suicide planes or Kamikazes ('**Divine Wind**') was discussed at high level for the first time and a Kamikaze Special Attack Force established and trained.

The first strikes by the Special Attack Force came on October 25/26 in Leyte Gulf, where 55 suicide planes succeeded in sinking the escort carrier St Lo and damaging six other carriers. The attacks were judged a success. The Force was greatly expanded and over 2,000 more Kamikaze attacks were launched by the end of the year.

Although a terrifying and bewildering prospect for the Allies to face, Kamikaze attacks failed to change very much in the grander scheme of things. A tactic to combat them, called '**The Big Blue Blanket**' saw fighter and naval picket ships develop a powerful screen against incoming targets and ship gunners developed effective new tactics for dealing with any that got through. Less than ten percent of Kamikazes that did get through caused enough damage to sink a ship, and losses were mostly confined to smaller ships such as destroyers.

RIGHT: Members of 72nd Shinbu Squadron. Three of the five are 17 years old and the other two are 18 and 19 years old OPPOSITE PAGE: A group of kamikaze pilots bowing

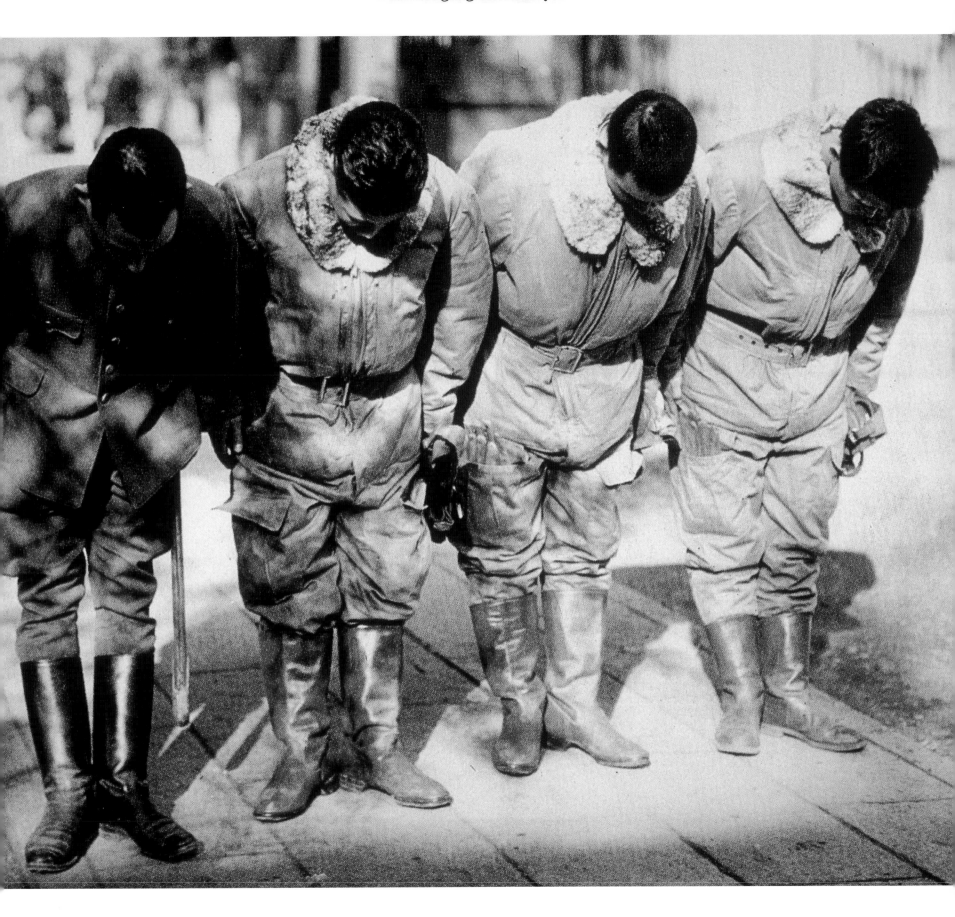

ABOVE: Members of the Special Attack Unit Kinno-tai sing songs before the kamikaze attack during the Battle of Leyte Gulf OPPOSITE PAGE;
BOTTOM LEFT: The crew of the Japanese aircraft carrier Zuikaku salute as the flag is lowered during the battle off Cape Engaño BOTTOM MIDDLE:
The Japanese carrier Zuiho pictured during the Battle of Cape Engano BOTTOM MIDDLE: The U.S. Navy motor torpedo boat PT-131 preparing for
the Battle of Surigao Strait

THE BATTLE OF LEYTE GULF

Japanese naval commanders had assessed that, if the Allies retook the Philippines, their own lines of supply would be almost completely severed. They would still have a relatively large naval fleet, but no way to refuel it or resupply it. They had only one solution. Come out and fight.

The Japanese split their ships into three forces. Northern Force, with its tempting aircraft carriers as bait would lure away the U.S. 3rd Fleet, while Center Force and Southern Force would sail for Leyte and destroy the Allied beachhead. What followed was the largest naval battle in history.

Center Force came to grief first. Comprising five battleships, 10 heavy cruisers, 2 light cruisers and 15 destroyers, it was found and attacked by two American submarines – the Darter and Dace – both firing full spreads of torpedoes into the unsuspecting fleet at dawn on October 23. The heavy cruiser – and flagship of the fleet - Atago was hit and sunk first, pitching the Japanese admiral in charge of Center Force into the ocean and forcing him to swim for his life. The heavy cruiser Maya was sunk next, and its fellow heavy cruiser Takao so badly damaged that it was forced to turn around and limp back to base. Attacks on Center Force continued the next day, when it was targeted by dive and torpedo bombers off the USS Enterprise. They were joined later by other combat aircraft off the carriers Intrepid, Cabot, Essex, Franklin and Lexington. After causing serious damage to the heavy cruiser Myoko and crippling the battleship Musashi (which later sank), the aircraft caused Center Force to turn around and flee out of range. In retaliation, the Japanese threw three waves of their land based bombers against the American carriers. Virtually all the Japanese planes were torn down by the carriers' fighter air cover but one Judy bomber managed to get through to the light carrier USS Princeton and cause so much damage that she later had to be scuttled. As night fell on October 24, Center Force changed course under cover of darkness and was inbound for Leyte once more.

Late in the afternoon of October 24, the Allies detected the carrier-rich Northern Force and just as the Japanese had hoped, sent the 3rd Fleet north to engage it. The chance to destroy so many carriers was just too tempting to miss.

On October 25, Southern Force arrived to link up with the badly mauled but still dangerous Centre Force. Southern Force comprised two battleships, three heavy cruisers, a light cruiser and eight destroyers. As it was trying to liaise with Center Force and co-ordinate a devastating attack on the American beachhead on Leyte, the Americans sprung their trap. Far from being undefended as Halsey set off in pursuit of the Japanese carrier fleet to the north, the 7th Fleet Support Force had been left to deal with them – and the 7th Fleet Support Force had six battleships, 4 heavy cruisers, 4 light cruisers, 28 destroyers and 39 little motor torpedo boats. The ships of Southern Force effectively found themselves running a gauntlet of American warships by night, with nippy little torpedo boats weaving in and out of the fleet and harassing the big ships. The grand old battleship Fuso was the first ship to be sunk, quickly followed by two Japanese destroyers. As the night progressed, the battleship Yamashiro was shelled into oblivion with the loss of the Southern Force commander. The surviving Japanese ships were firing wildly in all directions now, their fire control no match for the American

new radar system. The Japanese turned and fled, running blind.

The next day, fortunes changed. The Japanese Center Force caught an American fleet comprised of vulnerable escort carriers and destroyers unprepared for them. As the carriers fled under a smoke screen, the order was given, *'small boys attack!'* and the Allied support destroyers turned and steered straight for the mighty Kaigun fleet bearing down on them. They succeeded in disrupting the Japanese fleet and slowing them down, but at a terrible price. Now all 450 aircraft aboard the escort carriers were launched with whatever weapons they had on board to tangle with Center Force, buying them more valuable time to escape. Only one escort carrier was sunk in the engagement, blasted by the big guns of the super battleship Yamato. The sheer ferocity with which the light Allied fleet had fought back convinced the Japanese commander that he had encountered a much bigger Allied force than he really had. In genuine confusion, Center Fleet set out chasing after a non-existent major carrier force and did not attack Leyte after all. After that, mauled and bewildered, they retreated.

On October 25, the 3rd Fleet finally caught up with the Kaigun's Northern Force which comprised four aircraft carriers (but with few aircraft aboard thanks to lack of supply), 3 light carriers, two old battleships converted to carriers, 3 light cruisers and 9 destroyers. Halsey's plan was to attack them first from the air and then to shell them with the battleships' big guns. Before they could do that though, the Japanese managed to get 75 of their aircraft into the air to attack. Most were destroyed by the lethally efficient fighters of the fleet's carrier air cover and the few Japanese warplanes that did escape fled for land bases on Luzon. In return, Halsey's carriers let loose 180 aircraft aimed at the Japanese. The escort fighters ripped down the Japanese air cover, allowing the dive bombers and torpedo planes to really get in amongst the enemy shipping. In raids which lasted all day they sank the carrier Zuikaku (which had taken part in the raid on Pearl Harbor), two light carriers and a destroyer. Just as Halsey was preparing to send his battleships in for the kill, he got wind of the fighting down near Leyte and decided he had no choice but to turn around and defend the beachhead.

The Fleets disengaged. The Battle of Leyte Gulf was over. The Imperial Japanese navy had suffered stunning losses, which included one aircraft carrier, three light carriers and 3 battleships.

BOMBING JAPAN – THE FIRST RAIDS

The strategic bombing of Japan had started in earnest in June 1944. Codenamed Operation Matterhorn, it used new, long-range B-29s setting out from bases safely back in Bengal, India and working through forward bases in Free China for refuelling. From this remote position, the B-29s could only reach Kyushu, the southernmost of Japan's four main islands. Japan knew they would be coming and started withdrawing much-needed fighter aircraft from other parts of the Pacific to meet the threat at home. They also tried to embark on the building of public shelters, but waging such a far-ranging war had left them desperately short of steel and concrete. In the cities, largely made of wood and paper to minimise earthquake damage, there was a huge risk of uncontrolled firestorms breaking out after a bombing raid and giant firebreaks were constructed by pulling down peoples' houses. Over three million Japanese were made homeless, while women and children were evacuated to the countryside from those cities identified as being most likely to be bombed.

The B-29 raids, when they came, were made against industrial targets on Kyushu such as steelworks and aircraft factories. Nine raids were launched in all, but proved largely ineffectual. 125 B-29s were lost on the operations. Japanese anti-aircraft fire and fighter interceptors accounted for less than 25 of them. The rest were lost due to flying or mechanical error. The B-29 was still a very new and technically demanding aircraft, full of lethal teething problems. The raids ceased on January 6 1945 and at the beginning of April, the B-29 force in India relocated to the Marianas.

MAIN IMAGE: Female students work at the Imperial Japanese Army Kokura Armony BOTTOM LEFT: Aircrews of the 426th Night Fighter Squadron at their first operational base at Chengtu, China, 1944. From Chengtu, their mission was to protect B-29 Superfortresses using Chinese Air Bases as staging bases from India on Operation Matterhorn Missions to Japan BOTTOM MIDDLE: Twentieth Air Force B-29s at an airfield in India

FROM LEYTE TO VICTORY IN THE PHILIPPINES

Despite the Allied victory at Leyte Gulf, the Japanese were still able to send convoys into Leyte Island to reinforce its garrison and even dropped paratroopers on American-held airbases. (They were wiped out after an intense four day battle). It would be Christmas Day 1944 before the last resistance was crushed there, despite essential help from local Filipino guerrillas. American deaths numbered some 3,000, while the Japanese defenders took 56,000 casualties. A further 27,000 Japanese holdouts died during routine *'mopping up'* operations after Christmas.

Landings on the island of Mindoro had followed landings on Leyte. MacArthur planned to use its strategic position to launch airstrikes against the Japanese embedded in the Philippine capital Manila on the island of Luzon. Despite desperate attacks on the invasion fleet by Kamikazes, the landings on December 15 1944 were successful and the light Japanese presence on the island swiftly overwhelmed.

Landings on the main Philippines island of Luzon began on January 9 1945, with waves of Kamikazes sinking or damaging 25 ships. Nevertheless, within just a few days, 175,000 men of the U.S. 6th Army were ashore and heading for Manila in a pincer movement with other troops including paratroopers. 260,000 Japanese were waiting for them. The battle that followed took five months and cost the Americans 38,000 casualties. The Japanese lost 190,000 men. The fight for the capital Manila between February and March 1945 was even harsher than expected. During lulls in the fighting, the frightened and frustrated Japanese defenders conducted a series of atrocities in Manila schools, convents and hospitals. Women were seized and forced into the city's Bayview Hotel which the Japanese then designated a *'Rape Centre'*. Perhaps as many as half a million civilians died in Manila, most as a result of systematic Japanese atrocities, during its liberation.

Eventually, the Japanese Army regulars turned and fled but Japanese Navy Marines fought on with a desperate ferocity. The Japanese marines fought a last stand from Fort Drum, an island in Manila Bay. On April 13, U.S. Forces pumped 3,000 gallons of diesel into the fort and then ignited it with incendiaries. There were no survivors. After Manila was liberated, the U.S. 8th Army were brought in to conduct a number of *'clear up'* amphibious assaults on remaining Japanese positions in the southern Philippines.

EXPANDING THE BOMBING RAIDS

Once air bases on the Mariana Islands became available from November 1944, the bombing of Japan was greatly increased. The Marianas air bases could accommodate hundreds of B-29 and from their location, raiders could now reach Tokyo and indeed many other parts of the Home Islands previously inaccessible. Bombing raids on industrial targets in Tokyo had commenced at the end of November 1944 but – despite the fact that they were now safer and simpler to carry out – had little effect. Raids on Tokyo and on Nagoya (which was rich in aircraft manufacturing plants) continued until March 1945 with mixed but generally unsatisfactory results. The failure was put down to

ABOVE: General Douglas MacArthur, accompanied by Lieutenant General George C. Kenney, Lieutenant General Richard K. Sutherland and Major General Verne D. Mudge, speaks with troops on the beach, Leyte, Philippines, October 20, 1944 **BOTTOM LEFT:** The officers and men of the Cooper's Unit, Southern Mindoro Guerrilla Force, Bolo Area **BOTTOM MIDDLE:** Newly arrived USAAF Republic P-47 Thunderbolts in a maintenance area at Agana Airfield, Guam, Marianas Islands **BOTTOM RIGHT:** Tinian, Mariana Islands, after airfield construction, looking north to south

poor weather and visibility over the target and frequent mechanical problems with the B-29s, many of whom regularly had to turn back from missions because of faults with their aircraft (unexplained engine fires were an early problem of note). Something had to change.

THE LIBERATION OF BURMA

The Allies came in force in 1944 and the Japanese had no answer to it. The new, senior Japanese officer commanding, General Hyotaro Kimura, fell back from the Chindwin River and took up defensive positions behind the Irrawaddy River instead. The Allies had just one aim – to retake the capital Rangoon by May 1945 when the monsoons would make fighting nearly impossible.

Chinese forces made good progress in the north from December 1944, although weakened by the need to divert a significant portion of their resources back to China, where fighting had been intensifying. During January and February 1945, elements of the British 14th Army successfully captured several crossings over the Irrawaddy River and by March Mandalay returned to British control as the Japanese retreated still further. Other elements of the 14th fought their way south down the Irrawaddy and – after breaking strong Japanese resistance at Pyawbwe – found little between themselves and Rangoon, until they were halted by a rag-tag assemblage of whomever the Japanese could throw together to hold them 40 miles north of the capital. This bought the Japanese valuable time to evacuate from Rangoon. While the British finally broke through and headed south again, a combined India – Ghurka operation moved to join them in the seizing of the capital.

Japanese forces in other parts of Burma were still holding out and resisting by July 1945. The main Japanese force was effectively pinned down and when they did attempt a break out, it was a disaster. The British were ready for them all along the routes they had decided to use, while hundreds of Japanese soldiers died trying to navigate the swollen and wild Sittang River on cobbled together bamboo rafts. Stragglers who made it out were hunted down and murdered by ferocious Burmese Bandits. 10,000 men died trying to escape.

IWO JIMA – OPERATION DETACHMENT

'...the most savage and the most costly battle in the history of the Marine Corps'

Lieutenant-General Holland 'Howling Mad' Smith

Located half way between the Marianas and Downtown Tokyo, invading the tiny island of Iwo Jima must have seemed like a good idea at the time. It was home to three airfields, and the fighter aircraft on the island had been responsible for attacking U.S. bombers on missions

ABOVE RIGHT: Map of the Iwo Jima Landing Plan **OPPOSITE PAGE; TOP:** Poster for the Seventh War Loan Drive, depicting the raising of the flag on Iwo Jima

7th WAR LOAN NOW··ALL TOGETHER

OFFICIAL U. S. TREASURY POSTER

to Japan. Once neutralised and in American hands however, it could offer refuge for damaged B-29s limping their way back from raids over the Home Islands and act as a home base for their fighter escorts. Everyone knew it would be a tough fight, but it would be worth it.

Three U.S. Marine divisions stormed the eight mile square rock on February 19 1945 after its defenders had been softened up with an extended barrage that dropped 6,800 tons of bombs and 22,000 naval shells on the 23,000 Japanese soldiers defending the island. As had become the established pattern by now, the Japanese did not plan to hold the beaches but let the marines come on in. As on other islands, they had prepared elaborate defence networks of 11 miles of tunnels up to five levels deep, plus caves, bunkers, pill boxes, dug outs and hidden artillery emplacements. However, when the volcanic ash started bogging down the American vehicles and the beach became overcrowded with men and materials, the Japanese on Mount Suribachi could not resist shelling it and began to wreak havoc. The marines tried digging in but the ash just slid in all directions. To defend their men pinned down on the beaches, support ships moved in close and began returning fire at the Japanese artillery and mortar positions away to the north, desperately trying to suppress them. The landing force took 2,400 casualties on the first day, but pressed on.

The Americans found moving off the beaches difficult, as their own bombardment had churned up much of the landscape and littered it with crater and debris. Well-hidden Japanese snipers further held up their progress. By day 4, marines had secured Mount Suribachi, and were photographed raising the American flag over the island in what would become one of the most famous images of the entire war.

Beyond Suribachi still lay the strongest and best defended Japanese positions on high elevations and the marines had no choice but to go up the slopes and get in among them with bayonets, grenades and flamethrowers. They were supported by P-51 Mustang fighters operating now out of one of the airbases on the island, dropping bombs on the Japanese positions while Sherman tanks adapted to spray napalm burnt the Japanese out of their concealments. 70,000 Allied men ended up fighting on Iwo Jima and the end result was never seriously in doubt, but some Marine rifle companies suffered up to 75% casualties and officers and NCOs were killed and replaced so fast that often the men had no idea who was currently commanding them.

By March 26, the operation was declared over. It had been planned to last a week. It lasted over a month. 20,000 Japanese died defending their positions, while their commanders died either by their own hands or in futile Banzai charges straight into the American guns. The U.S. Marines suffered 24,053 men killed or wounded – more than the Japanese casualties. This was the first time this had happened – and it shocked the Allied commanders as well as the American public when news reached home. If one tiny – and relatively unimportant - volcanic rock in the middle of nowhere could claim so many lives, what would happen when the Allies took on a target more important to the Japanese?

MAIN IMAGE: Iwo Jima - another wave of US Marines moves in **ABOVE:** Iwo Jima Historical Map **OPPOSITE PAGE; BOTTOM LEFT:** U.S. Navy Grumman TBM Avenger over Iwo Jima **BOTTOM MIDDLE:** US Marines on their way to Iwo Jima **BOTTOM RIGHT:** USS Alaska, Crew of a 40mm quad anti aircraft machine gun mount loading clips into the loaders of the left pair of guns, during the Iwo Jima operation

ABOVE: Out of the gaping mouths of Coast Guard and Navy Landing Craft, rose the great flow of invasion supplies to the blackened sands of Iwo Jima, a few hours after the Marines had wrested their foothold on the vital island

ABOVE: A Marine flame throwing tank, also known as a "Ronson", scorches a Japanese strongpoint. The eight M4A3 Shermans equipped with the Navy Mark 1 flame-thrower proved to be the most valuable weapons systems on Iwo Jima

ABOVE: An observer who spotted a machine gun nest finds its location on a map so they can send the information to artillery or mortars to wipe out the position. Iwo Jima

ABOVE: Private First Class Rez P. Hester, 7th War Dog Platoon, 25th Regiment, takes a nap while Butch, his war dog, stands guard. Iwo Jima

The Setting Sun

FIRE RAIDS

'Hell could be no hotter'

Robert Guillain, reporter

In January 1945, Major-General Curtis LeMay took over air operations and formed the XX Air Force. Whilst in Europe he had seen German cities burn. With the obvious failure of precision bombing on Japan, he now decided to firebomb the flimsy paper cities by night with B-29s flying low at 5,000 feet rather than at their usual ceiling of 30,000 feet. USAAF knew the damage could be enormous and they had estimates that up to half a million civilians might die, but by now – like most Americans - they just wanted the war over and done with. The atrocities the Americans had seen the Japanese commit right across the Pacific had hardened them, and they had begun to see all Japanese – military and civilians alike - as terrible and only worthy of extermination. Let them all burn then.

Just before dawn on March 10 1945, a force of 279 B-29s began to arrive over Tokyo. They had been stripped of all non-essential weight, including their guns, to be able to carry even more bombs than usual. They dropped payloads of M69 napalm-based incendiary cluster bombs and succeeded in starting fires that would kill up to 100,000 people and injure another 40,000 as 16 square miles of the city was consumed in flames. Civil defences were overwhelmed and the firebreaks proved totally inadequate compared to the scale of the conflagration. A million survivors were rendered homeless. Just 14 B-29s were lost on the raid.

Similar attacks followed throughout March 1945 against Nagoya, Osaka and Kobe and only stopped when the USAAF ran out of incendiary bombs. Although none of the other cities suffered as much as Tokyo had in the initial fire bombing, all the raids were judged successful. Fresh attacks against 22 Japanese cities were planned. These were largely delayed until May 1945 as the bomber force was redirected to support the invasion of Okinawa.

By the beginning of May 1945, the strength of the B-29 force in the Marianas had grown to just over 1,000 aircraft. Fresh firebombing raids were now launched against Japan's major cities, often with the protection of P-51 fighter escorts out of Iwo Jima by day and P-61 Black Widows by night. Tokyo and Nagoya burned again, along with Yokohama. Half of Tokyo was destroyed by now and the city was removed from the target list because there was nothing worth bombing there anymore. In just one month 1/7th of Japan's total urban area was destroyed from the air. Raids continued in June, hitting Osaka, Kobe and Amagasaki. Japanese casualties in just the two months were put at as high as 125,000 dead. By mid-June, USAAF was ready to target the smaller and mostly undefended Japanese cities. 25 of them were scheduled for destruction – four every night on a typical night. The raids carried on into July and then August, along with leaflet drops telling the Japanese to surrender. They didn't.

REVENGE

American B-29 aircrews unfortunate enough to be brought down over Japan could often expect little mercy. Of the 545 pilots and crew captured by the Japanese, 132 were later executed by the authorities and 30 murdered by civilians. 94 more men died while in captivity. Eight were subjected to vivisection by the professors at Kyushu Imperial University.

OPPOSITE PAGE; **TOP:** US air bombardment of Japan is disrupted as a Japanese bomb explodes underneath a US aircraft. July 1945 **BOTTOM LEFT:** Rescuing buried people after a Tokyo raid **BOTTOM MIDDLE:** Bodies litter the streets of Tokyo, March 1945 **BOTTOM RIGHT:** Devastation of Tokyo, March 1945

OKINAWA — OPERATION ICEBERG

Okinawa, in the Ryukyu Islands, had only been officially part of Japan since 1879, when it was *'annexed'* by the Home Islands. By 1945, the Okinawans were considered to be *'Japanese but not Japanese'*. They were Japanese when it suited the Japanese for them to be considered so. Despite Okinawa being only 350 miles away from Japan *'proper'*, they were ethnically different to those on the Home Islands and so were both considered an ethnic minority and deeply inferior as a race. Now, they would be expected to stand fast and to sacrifice everything they had for Japan proper as the Allies moved in to invade. It was the perfect place to fight a grinding, vicious war of attrition, the Japanese High Command decided, since the people caught up in the horror would not be *'proper'* Japanese.

The Allies knew they needed Okinawa as both an advanced air base and a staging post for their intended invasion of the Japanese Home Islands – but taking it would be a daunting task. The casualties suffered seizing tiny Iwo Jima had come as a rude shock – and Okinawa was vast compared to the usual island the Allies had targeted in the past – some 60 miles long and 18 miles wide in places. Bombardment was restricted by the presence of half a million civilians and the Japanese defences – four lines of pillboxes, caves, underground facilities and bunkers bristling with artillery and mortars - showed that the Japanese were prepared to mount a fierce and determined delaying campaign which would lay waste to Okinawa while the Home Islands that mattered built ever-better defences. As far as the Japanese authorities believed, nothing on Okinawa was beyond sacrifice.

On Easter Sunday, April 1 1945, two marine divisions and two infantry divisions landed on the northern beaches of Okinawa, facing 100,000 men of the Imperial Japanese 32nd army as well as 9,000 sailors from the Kaigun and 40,000 native Okinawans conscripted into a rough militia. Of these, 2,000 were just schoolboys – some as young as 14. They were given the grand name of the **'Iron and Blood Imperial Corps'**.

No one was fooled by now when the landing forces met no opposition and the Allies were allowed to take rapid control of most of the north of the island. The Japanese were just waiting for them to come south and onto the kill zones they had established in front of their lines of defence…

ABOVE: US Marines run and jump for cover as they disembark from the LVTs in which they came ashore, Okinawa, Japan, April 1945 **OPPOSITE PAGE; TOP:** F6F-5N Hellcat is launched from the escort carrier USS Block Island off Okinawa on 10 May 1945 **BOTTOM LEFT:** Bombarding Okinawa with her 14"/50 main battery guns, as LVTs carry troops to the invasion beaches **BOTTOM MIDDLE:** Aerial view of Bolo airfield, Okinawa **BOTTOM RIGHT:** Explosive device concealed in a head of cabbage, Okinawa. Such booby traps were prevalent and highly dangerous

THE KAMIKAZE WAR

In support of the fighting on Okinawa, 13 aircraft carriers were kept on station off the east coast as part of Task Force 58. A Commonwealth fighting force comprised of 4 British aircraft carriers and 6 escort carriers provided further cover from the south.

At first the naval units were largely ignored but everyone knew it couldn't last. On April 6, 400 Japanese warplanes from the island of Kyushu launched a heavy bombing raid. From that date until the third week of June 1945, almost 2,000 Kamikazes poured out of Kyushu and Formosa. Although they did not succeed in sinking any of the important Allied warships, they did succeed in getting through to the carriers and damaging several of them.

ABOVE: Firefighters aboard the aircraft carrier USS *Hancock* hosing down damage caused by a Japanese kamikaze attack

THE YAMATO PUTS TO SEA

The fight for Okinawa was considered so critical that the Japanese threw their most advanced and prized battleship, the Yamato, into the fray. Under the command of Admiral Seiichi Itō, she would sail as part of a ten ship fleet for Okinawa. The plan was to fight her way through the Allied naval blockade and then to beach herself along with any other surviving Japanese warships. Their big guns would then be used to bombard American forces on the island while the crews disembarked and fought as regular Japanese soldiers. The efficacy of this odd plan was never put to the test. The Yamato and her escorts were swarmed by over 300 Allied dive and torpedo bombers from the carriers operating in the region. The battleship Yamato was sunk at sea along with five of her escorts and almost 4,000 Japanese sailors were killed including Admiral Ito himself. The Allies lost just ten aircraft.

ABOVE: Japanese battleship Yamato under construction at the Kure Naval Base, Japan

OKINAWA — FIGHT TO THE FINISH

American forces reached the first of the Southern defence lines on April 6 and their rapid advance came to an abrupt and total halt. On April 19, the Americans attacked in force, supported by a staggering 27 artillery battalions and 375 aircraft. Despite this they made next to no progress. The Japanese defenders simply went underground during the bombardments and then returned to their positions once it was safe. The fight was deadlocked. Still having strong reserves, the Japanese commander General Ushijima decided to use many of them in a daring counterattack which included amphibious landings behind American lines. Due to a series of blunders the Japanese did not come ashore where they had intended and were held and driven off by alert U.S. troops. At dawn the next day, heavy Japanese forces surged from their lines towards the Allied troops but were broken by artillery and close air support. The Japanese lost close to 7,000 men in the action, but because they had been reserves, their defensive lines were still at full strength.

Between the start of May and early June, fighting on Okinawa degenerated into a grim war of attrition as the Americans attacked and the Japanese staunchly defended, falling back from one defensive line as It weakened to the next. Very little changed but the casualty figures kept climbing and, while the Americans could bring in fresh reinforcements onto the island, the Japanese were limited to the men they had in place. Now the (racially inferior) children of the **'Iron and Blood Imperial Corps'** were sacrificed in suicide attacks against

ABOVE: US Marine charging Japanese Machine Guns on Okinawa **OPPOSITE PAGE; TOP:** Soldier is removed from the tank which carried him from the front. Japanese artillery and small arms fire made it impossible for ambulances to carry the wounded to the rear. Okinawa, 1945 **BOTTOM LEFT:** Marines pass through a small village where Japanese soldiers lay dead. Okinawa **BOTTOM MIDDLE:** A Marine of the 1st Marine Division takes aim on a Japanese sniper on Wana Ridge, Shuri. Okinawa **BOTTOM RIGHT:** Japanese prisoners of war at Okuku, Okinawa

U.S. tanks or on hopeless guerrilla missions.

By the end of May, monsoon rains turned the battlefield into a quagmire of filth more reminiscent of the worst of the Western Front battles of the First World War than anything else. It became impossible to bury the dead or even to retrieve them from the field. They were left to sink into the liquid mud. Soldiers fighting on the battlefield would complain of being covered in maggots whenever they lay down, fresh from the rotting corpses strewn everywhere. American soldiers at the front began to show signs of **'shell shock'**, another throwback to the Great War.

By June 16, Japanese defences started to crumble at last and - realising defeat was near - the Japanese commander instructed his remaining forces to break up and fight on as guerrilla units. He would commit suicide a few days later, just as the American commanders were claiming victory on the island.

Over 12,000 American soldiers died taking Okinawa and a further 50,000 were wounded. The Japanese dead exceeded 150,000 including many civilians. As many as 1/3rd of the civilian population perished in the fighting. No-one was sure. Some of the Okinawans had fled to caves to hide from the fighting, and these had then been blocked by shelling, entombing them alive. During the Japanese soldiers' retreat from one defensive line to another, they had ruthlessly plundered any civilian homes they could find for food and drink – and women. Some civilians starved. Those who resisted were murdered, as were over 1,000 Okinawans loosely suspected of **'spying'**. More Okinawans were killed when the soldiers used them as human shields. As they fell back, the soldiers told the Okinawans stories of how the advancing Americans

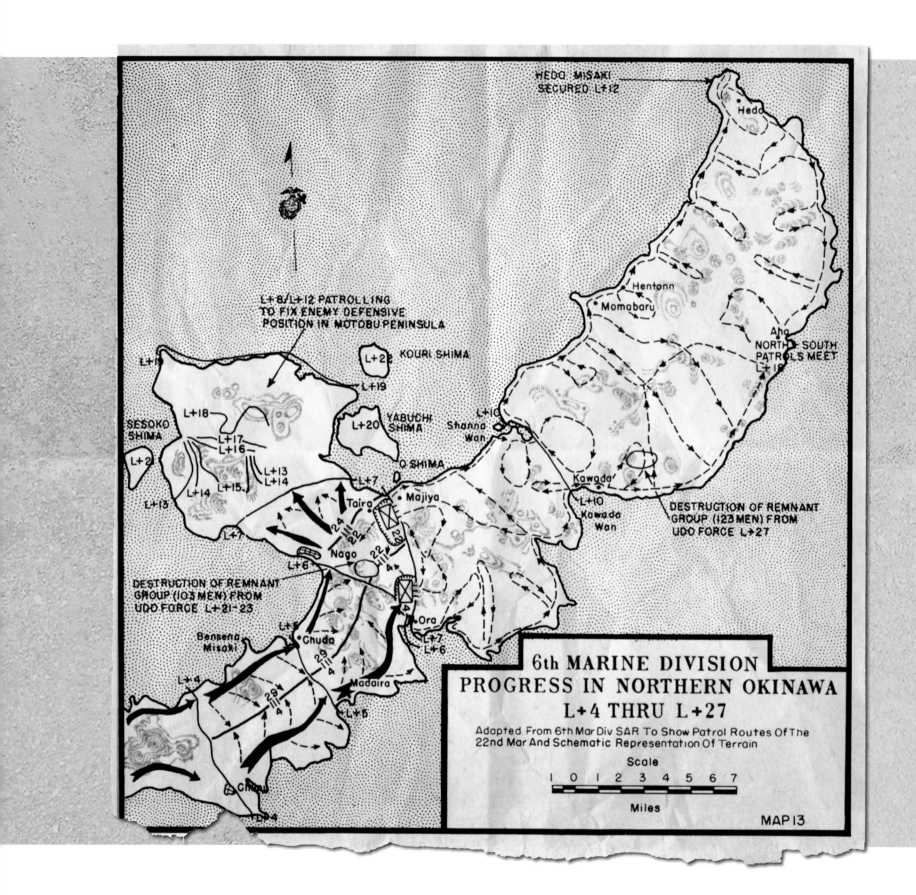

HEDO MISAKI
SECURED L+12

Hedo

L+8/L+12 PATROLLING
TO FIX ENEMY DEFENSIVE
POSITION IN MOTOBU PENINSULA

Hentona

Momobaru

Aha
NORTH – SOUTH
PATROLS MEET
L+19

KOURI SHIMA
L+2?
L+19

SESOKO
SHIMA
L+18
L+17
L+16

YABUCHI
SHIMA
L+20
Shanna
Wan
L+10

O SHIMA

Kawada
Kawada
Wan
L+10

DESTRUCTION OF REMNANT
GROUP (123 MEN) FROM
UDO FORCE L+27

L+2
L+13
L+14 L+15
L+13 L+14
L+7
Taira
L+7
Majiya

24
22
2/29

Nago
22
4/1

DESTRUCTION OF REMNANT
GROUP (103 MEN) FROM
UDO FORCE L+21-23

L+6

L+5
Bensena
Misaki
Chuda
29
4/1

Ora
L+7
L+6

Madaira

L+4
29
4/1

L+5

Chibu
L+4

6th MARINE DIVISION
PROGRESS IN NORTHERN OKINAWA
L+4 THRU L+27

Adapted From 6th Mar Div SAR To Show Patrol Routes Of The
22nd Mar And Schematic Representation Of Terrain

Scale

1 0 1 2 3 4 5 6 7

Miles

MAP 13

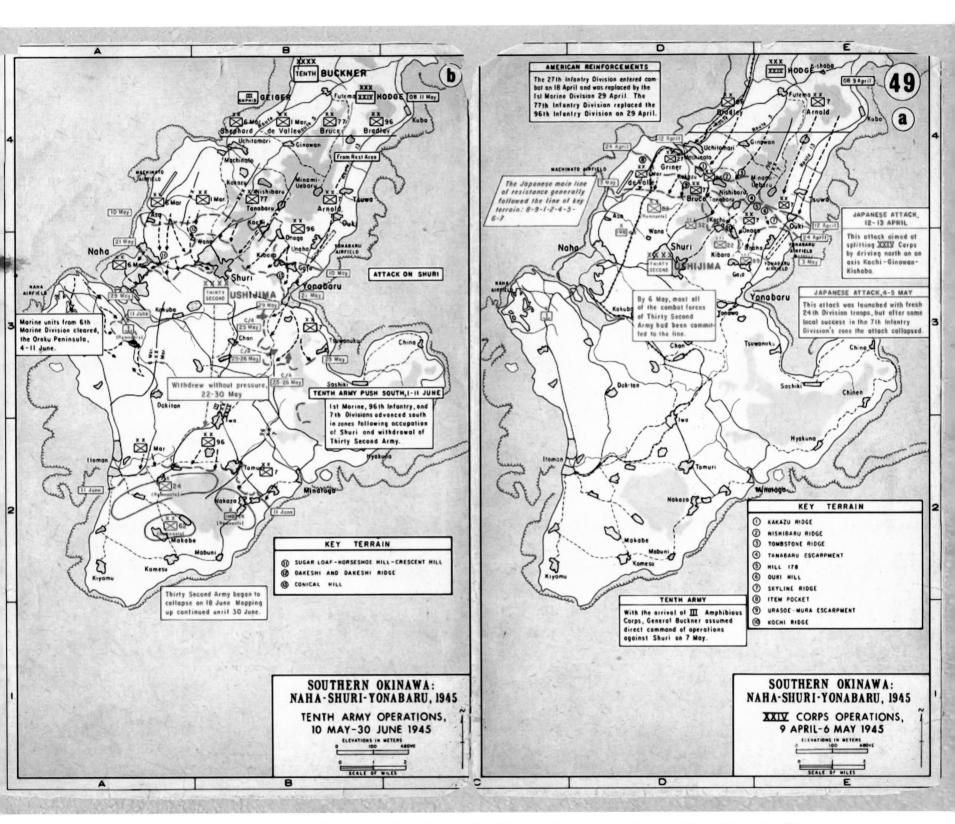

ABOVE: Maps showing the advance of the Marines in southern Okinawa : the 49th table is the advance between April 9 and May 6 , the 49b advance table between May 10 and June 30 **OPPOSITE PAGE:** Advance of the 6th Marines Division in northern Okinawa

ABOVE: Japanese POWs who gave themselves up at Kerama-retto

ABOVE: Battle Weary-Marines of a Sixth Division mortar crew snatch forty winks after a hard night of fighting for the capital city of Naha

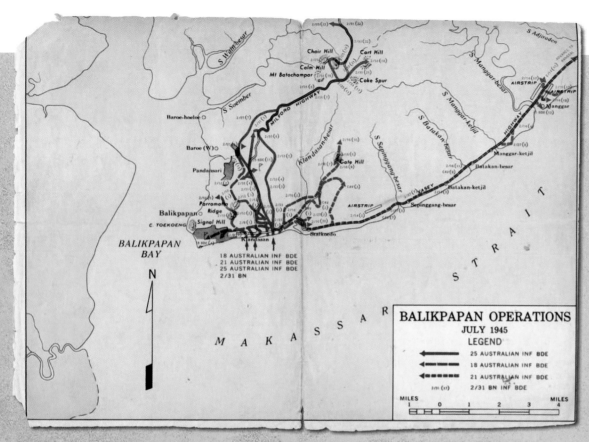

would rape and then possibly eat their captives. They then gave out hand grenades so that entire families could blow themselves up, all wrapped around a single grenade. Other families committed suicide by jumping together from the high cliffs on the south coast.

Once more, the Allied High Command was deeply troubled by the casualty figures. What would an invasion of the Home Islands cost in terms of American lives, and indeed in the number of Japanese civilians dead if the horrors repeated themselves on island after island? They started doing the math...and didn't like the answer they got.

RETAKING BORNEO

The decision to retake Borneo was a controversial one. The island had been left thus far to **'wither on the vine'** and the critical thrust of the Allied war effort had moved on to the fringes of the Japanese Home Islands thousands of miles away. While Borneo had once been an important source for oil for the Japanese, the seas around the island were now completely in Allied hands and it could no longer be

shipped back to Japan. Allies looking at the island in May 1945 saw an opportunity to gain access to that oil – and to free thousands of Allied POWs held on Borneo. MacArthur also permitted the campaign as a way to raise the profile of Australia's contribution to the war effort, after passing over Australian troops in favour of Americans during the retaking of the Philippines

The Australians first landed on the small, oil-rich island of Tarakan off the northeast coast of Borneo on May 1. They met fierce resistance from Japanese guarding the island's main airstrip, but eventually took it on May 5 only to find it had been heavily damaged by the Allies' initial bombardment prior to landing. Other airstrips on the island had been similarly knocked out. Japanese troops fled first to the rugged centre of the island but could not hold out against Allied artillery and the big guns of warships at sea and finally fled off the island to neighbouring Borneo in mid-June.

The Australian 9th Division and American troops landed at Brunei in mid-June and the Japanese defenders fled. More Australian landings followed at Balikpapan in southeast Borneo and met similarly weak resistance. The Japanese 37th Army finally surrendered on September 10 1945.

Few Allied POWs were rescued. Aware that the Allies were closing in and might invade, the Japanese sent their captives (Mostly Australian, though some British) on a series of **'Death Marches'** moving them from Sandakan to a more secure location at Ranau deeper into the interior. Those too weak to travel were killed in their camps. Those who fell as they marched were shot or bayoneted. On the second series of death marches, of the 536 POWs who set out, only 183 reached their destination alive. On the final march, forced on 75 POWs, all died before the march had got 30 miles out from its departure point. Those who did make it to their destination soon began to die from disease and starvation. Some met an even more terrible fate too as their Japanese captors resorted to cannibalism to survive the Allied blockade. The final 38 survivors were

ABOVE: Map of the Balikpapan Operations, July 1945 **OPPOSITE PAGE:** A Coast Guard combat photographer snaps Australian troops as they storm ashore in the first assault wave to hit Balikpapan on the Southeast Coast of Borneo. Heavy black smoke from burning oil wells can be seen from the beach. Balikpapen, Kalimantan, Indonesia

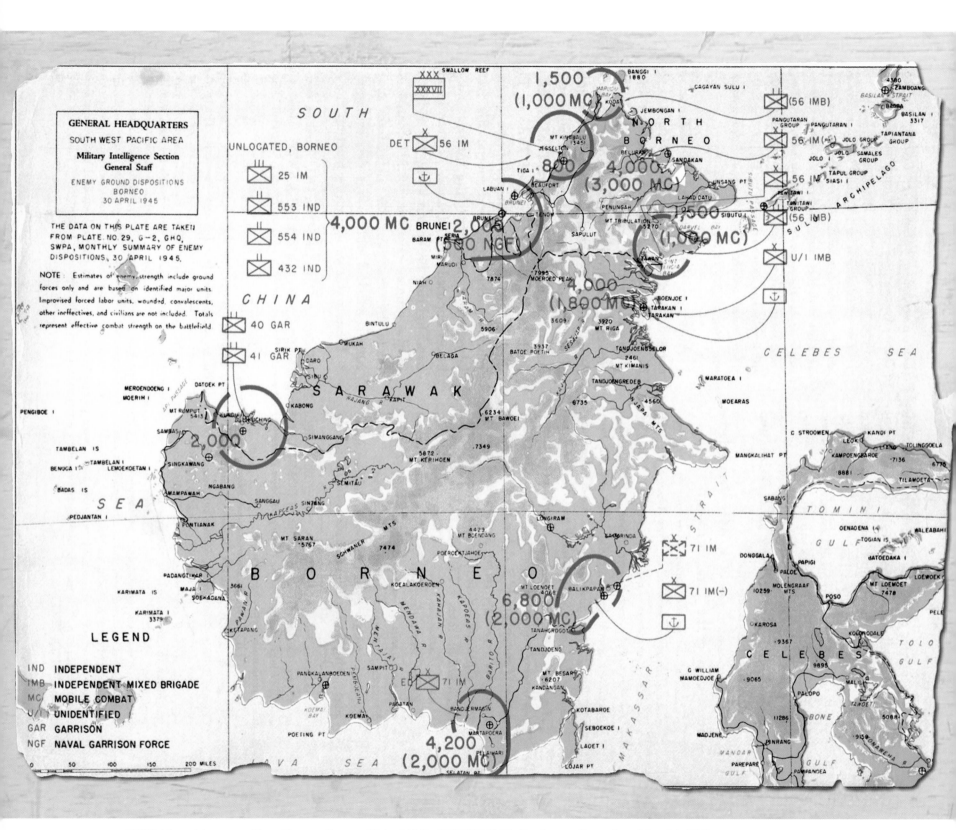

SOUTH

CHINA

SEA

CELEBES SEA

SARAWAK

BORNEO

CELEBES

JAVA SEA

GENERAL HEADQUARTERS
SOUTH WEST PACIFIC AREA
Military Intelligence Section
General Staff
ENEMY GROUND DISPOSITIONS
BORNEO
30 APRIL 1945

THE DATA ON THIS PLATE ARE TAKEN
FROM PLATE. NO. 29, G-2, GHQ,
SWPA, MONTHLY SUMMARY OF ENEMY
DISPOSITIONS, 30 APRIL 1945.

NOTE : Estimates of enemy strength include ground
forces only and are based on identified major units.
Improvised forced labor units, wounded, convalescents,
other ineffectives, and civilians are not included. Totals
represent effective combat strength on the battlefield.

UNLOCATED, BORNEO

25 IM

553 IND

554 IND

432 IND

40 GAR

41 GAR

LEGEND

IND   INDEPENDENT
IMB   INDEPENDENT MIXED BRIGADE
MC   MOBILE COMBAT
U/I   UNIDENTIFIED
GAR   GARRISON
NGF   NAVAL GARRISON FORCE

0   50   100   150   200 MILES

1,500
(1,000 MC)

800

4,000
(3,000 MC)

1,500

4,000 MC   BRUNEI 2,000
(500 NGF)

4,000
(1,800 MC)

1,500
(1,000 MC)

2,000

6,800
(2,000 MC)

4,200
(2,000 MC)

ABOVE: Map of Japanese Dispositions on Borneo, 30 April 1945   **OPPOSITE PAGE:** The Borneo Operations, May-July 1945

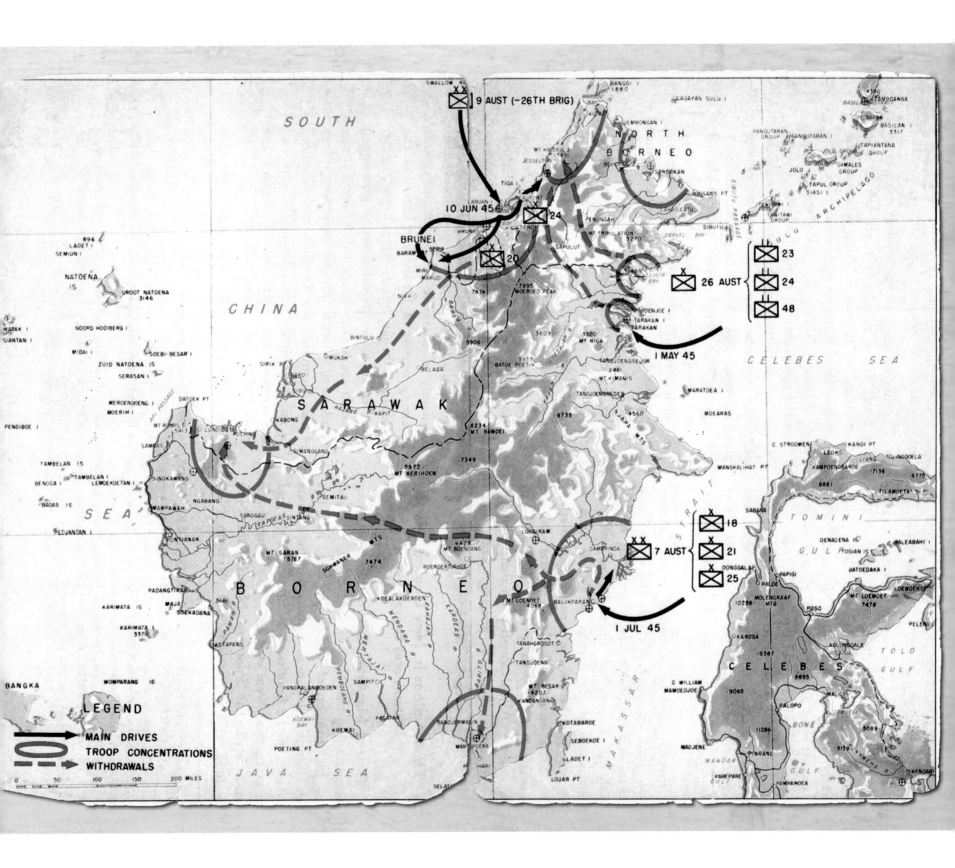

shot by their guards almost two weeks after the war had officially finished. Of the estimated 2,500 POWs interred at Sandakan, just six survived the war. Three low ranking Japanese officers were subsequently brought to justice at war crimes trials and were executed for the crimes committed during the death marches. The commandant of Kuching & Sandakan POW Camps, Colonel Suga, was captured but committed suicide whilst a prisoner by stabbing himself in the throat and then having his batman shatter his skull with a weighted water bottle.

SECRET PEACE MOVES

While the Japanese deliberately showed no interest in peace talks with the Allies, in secret they were talking to the Russians as a possible broker of peace terms throughout June of 1945. In particular, the Supreme Council for the Direction of the War (who were now running the country) under Prime Minister Admiral Kantarō Suzuki wanted to ensure that the Emperor would not be torn down and humiliated, and that Japan would not have to agree to *'Unconditional Surrender'*. They wanted most of all to save face.

The Supreme Council itself was split. The civilian members tended to want surrender on favourable and honourable terms. The military men wanted one last cataclysmic fight that would be so terrible that the Allies would accept peace almost on Japanese terms after the dust had settled.

By late June, with the loss of Okinawa, the Emperor himself called a Council meeting and told them that he desired an end to the war. To this

end he commanded that more talks be held with the Soviets. Despite continuing through the first half of July 1945, the talking went nowhere – and the Japanese had no idea that Russia was about to turn on them.

THE WITHERING OF JAPAN

Flying from carriers and newly captured air bases in the Ryukyu Islands from June 1945, American raiders pounded coastal shipping working between the Home Islands, severely disrupting the Japanese attempts to prepare for invasion. Bombers laid mines in Japanese waters, eventually succeeding in closing the harbors at Tokyo, Yokohama and Nagoya as part of what was unsubtly codenamed Operation Starvation.

In early July, a carrier-based Allied task force sailed into Japanese Home Island waters and began launching its bombers against airfields and coastal shipping as well as industrial targets. Joined by a British carrier fleet, they intensified their attacks on naval dockyards and any concentration of enemy warships potentially posing a threat to any forthcoming invasion force.

As Japanese resistance to the big B-29 raids crumbled, their P-51 escorts from Iwo Jima were freed up to strafe and attack Japanese airfields and to hunt and shoot up Japanese trains or lorry convoys wherever they could find them. They were later joined by P-47 Thunderbolts now flying out of the conquered island of Okinawa. Allied submarines prowled almost at will through Japan's coastal waters, raiding cargo ships plying their trade between the Home Islands and – by July 1945 – almost bringing the entire Japanese supply system to ruin.

ABOVE: Planes Over Fuji. B-29 Superfortresses over snow-covered Mount Fuji, Japan's sacred mountain, en route to Tokyo **BOTTOM LEFT:** Australian infantrymen taking cover behind a Matilda II tank while it fires on Japanese positions, Labuan **BOTTOM MIDDLE:** An Australian infantry company signalling position on Labuan, 26 June 1945 **BOTTOM RIGHT:** Japanese admiral Kantarō Suzuki

INVADING JAPAN

By now detailed Allied plans had been drawn up for the proposed invasion of the Japanese Home Islands, with MacArthur commanding ground forces and Nimitz the naval units. Unsubtly codenamed Operation Downfall, the invasion called for two separate but linked operations. Operation Olympic would see the Allies stream out of Okinawa and land on the largest southernmost island of the chain, Kyushu. This was scheduled for November 1 1945 and would require the largest naval fleet ever assembled – one comprising 42 aircraft carriers, 24 battleships and many hundreds of other warships and supply ships. 14 American divisions of the 6TH Army would storm 34 different beaches. The Allies were only intending to occupy one third of the island and establish huge air bases there. These air bases would then provide essential air support for the next stage of Downfall, Operation Coronet.

Operation Coronet was a planned mass amphibious landing on the island of Honshu close to Tokyo itself on March 1 1946. If it went ahead, it would be three and a half times larger than the D-Day landings of 1944 and up to 40 U.S. and Commonwealth divisions were thought necessary to take part in the initial landings or follow-up operations. Britain would supply around 25% of the close air support needed from its 18 carriers in the region and also from captured runways on Okinawa. There was talk of flying in the RAF's elite 617 **'Dambusters'** squadron to drop giant **'Grand Slam'** bombs on targets.

It was a fairly obvious plan, and the Japanese anticipated it completely. They planned to reinforce the southern end of Kyushu with virtually everything they had – and then dare the Allies to come on.

Supporting the land forces would be ten thousand Kamikazes, which would be all be directed towards the troop ships and supply vessels rather than the big warships as off Okinawa. In this way, they hoped to maximise Allied troops casualties before anyone even reached the beachheads. Waves of submarines and suicide boats would also target the Allied fleet, while what was left of the Kaigun would fight a defensive battle to the very last sailor.

The Japanese then called up a staggering 28 million civilian men and women from teenagers to pensioners to join the Patriotic Citizens Fighting Corps. They were to be poorly armed – sometimes with just bamboo poles or gardening implements – but they would still be useful if for nothing else than absorbing enemy bullets. Everything was planned to cause such high casualties that the allies would halt their invasion and settle for generous (to the Japanese) peace terms.

By July 1945, the number of Japanese infantry stationed on Kyushu was estimated to be in the region of 350,000 – and increasing rapidly. American planners thought it was entirely possible for there to be as many as 545,000 defenders dug in and in place by early August. And the invasion wasn't scheduled until November.

The Allied High Command started to become divided over the viability of Downfall. MacArthur and the Army wanted to press ahead but Admirals Nimitz and King were starting to have grave doubts. To back up their contrasting positions, everyone tried to come up with estimated casualty figures. One estimate predicted half a million American dead. Another Army estimate put the casualty figure at 400,000 dead and wounded – just from the invasion of Kyushu. A study done for Department of War estimated 1.7 to 4 million American casualties (with

ABOVE: Japanese city of Yokohama after the 'Great Yokohama Air Raid' of 29th May 1945. A third of the city was destroyed when US B.29 Superfortress bombers attacked the city with incendiary bombs, killing an estimated seven to eight thousand people **BOTTOM LEFT:** US President Harry S Truman **BOTTOM MIDDLE:** Nagoya after bombing **BOTTOM RIGHT:** General Douglas MacArthur und Admiral Chester W. Nimitz discuss tactics

800,000 dead) by the time Japan fell. Estimates of Japanese civilians who would die were considered as anywhere between 5 to 10 million, as they were expected to fight for their nation with fanatical zeal.

It became more and more clear to President Harry Truman that the estimates of American dead would never be acceptable to the American people. The administration was horrified too at the sheer number of Japanese civilians who would be slaughtered during Downfall. It would amount to a form of genocide. There were no good options.

There was only the least worst option.

THE LEAST WORST OPTION

After being in office for just a few months following the death of President Roosevelt in mid-April 1945, President Truman was asked to make one of the hardest decisions ever set before an American president. Should he sacrifice the lives of hundreds of thousands – perhaps millions – of American servicemen to subdue Japan? 418,000 Americans had died in World War Two thus far. Could he allow that number to double, or triple, in a final bloody cataclysm? Should he give orders which would mean the killing of millions of Japanese civilians? Should he allow an entire nation to be ground into dust? Should he listen to some of his commanders and start using poison gas on cities? Conventional bombing hadn't brought the Japanese to surrender even as their cities were pulverised and burned. The Navy's alternative plan for an indefinite blockade could see mass starvation on the Home Islands and the war stretching on for many years – and everyone was so sick and tired of war. War was no abstraction to Truman. He had seen it up close and at first hand, as an officer commanding an artillery battery during the Great War. The experience had not turned him into a war lover.

Truman had only been fully briefed about America's atomic bomb project on April 24 1945 – less than a fortnight after being sworn in. Up until then, so secret was the project that even the Vice President of the United States had no inkling of its existence. He had barely digested its full implications by July 16, when the very first nuclear bomb was successfully exploded at Trinity Test Site in New Mexico.

Truman both understood and did not understand what the Atom Bomb really was. His initial briefing papers referred to it as *'...in all probability...the most terrible weapon ever known in human history'* but then American bombers were already doing terrible things to Japanese cities on an industrial scale. This was just one big bomb doing the work of many smaller bombs, still free of political, moral or racial concerns and of any real understanding of radioactivity and radiation sickness.

When he had first been briefed, Truman had responded by setting up an Interim Committee to advise him on the matter. Now they were advising him to use the Atom Bomb on Japan as soon as was possible. It was a view he had come to share. He was petitioned not to use the bomb by a group of scientists and academics almost at the last minute, but found their moralising and speculating to be completely fanciful and at odds with any consideration of real world conditions.

Truman nevertheless decided to give Japan one last chance...

THE POTSDAM DECLARATION

On July 17 1945, President Truman met with British Prime Minister Winston Churchill and Soviet leader Josef Stalin at Potsdam in occupied Germany. While most of their attention was on matters relating to the fall of Nazi Germany, it was impossible to ignore the fact that the Allies (with the exception of the Soviet Union) were still fighting a war with Japan. On July 26, Truman and the new British Prime Minister Clement Attlee (who had replaced Churchill), together with the Chinese nationalist leader Chiang Kai-shek released The Potsdam Declaration – essentially the terms of surrender that they would accept from Imperial Japan. The terms were non-negotiable, the Allies announced: *'We will not deviate from them. There are no alternatives. We shall brook no delay.'* The terms called for the dismantling of existing Japanese structures of authority and the disarming of all Japanese forces. There would be retribution against *'war criminals'*, the surrender of occupied territories and strict limits on the nation's industries which would prevent them from rearming. And, as the document said at the end, it would mean *'unconditional surrender'*.

Japan did not respond, and two days later one of its most influential news sources referred to the Potsdam Declaration as a *'laughable matter'*.

LEFT: L to R: British Prime Minister Winston Churchill, President Harry S. Truman, and Soviet leader Josef Stalin in the garden of Cecilienhof Palace before meeting for the Potsdam Conference in Potsdam, Germany

HIROSHIMA

In the early hours of August 6 1945, the B-29 Enola Gay from 509th Composite Group took off out of North Field, Tinian. On board was an atomic bomb, codenamed Little Boy. Flying time to Japan was six hours. Over Iwo Jima, the Enola Gay rendezvoused with two more B-29s – The Great Artiste and Necessary Evil. They would photograph the bombing. Ahead of them a further B-29 - Straight Flush – was already providing reports on the weather conditions over Hiroshima.

Hiroshima was regarded as both an important industrial and military target. Several army headquarters were stationed there as well as significant amounts of troops. The population numbered some 350,000 and the city had been virtually untroubled by the fire raids to date. Most of the population considered themselves very lucky indeed. On the morning of the raid, Japanese radar saw the three B-29s approaching. It didn't look like a serious air attack and so the all-clear was sounded. People emerged from their shelters into the early morning sunshine.

The Enola Gay began its bomb run at nine minutes past eight in the morning. Six minutes later it released Little Boy. As it fell, the bomb was battered by crosswinds and so missed its intended detonation point.

That hardly mattered. The bomb misfired too. Only 1.38% of its Uranium fissiled - but that was more than enough. Little Boy exploded with a force of 16 kilotons in an air burst at 1,900 feet above the ground. There was a flash ten times as bright as the sun and almost instantly, the air temperature at the epicentre rose to over a million degrees Celsius.

The Enola Gay was 12 miles away when it was buffeted by the shock wave from the blast. To the rear, a mushroom cloud was rising. From his position in the rear turret, Staff Sergeant George Caron described what he saw.

'The mushroom cloud itself was a spectacular sight, a bubbling mass of purple-gray smoke and you could see it had a red core in it and everything was burning inside. . . . It looked like lava or molasses covering a whole city. . .'

The mushroom cloud would eventually extend to 40,000 feet in the air – 10,000 feet higher than the fleeing aircraft. Below, metal and stone alike had melted. Birds exploded into flames in mid-air. Those people closest to the blast were simply vaporised. All that remained were their shadows cast onto blasted walls.

70% of all the buildings in Hiroshima were destroyed in the blast and the firestorm which followed, consuming the flimsy timber and paper dwellings. No-one is quite sure how many died. 80,000 – 100,000 is a common estimate. This included 20,000 soldiers stationed in the city. Many thousands more would die later, from chronic radiation poisoning. Another 140,000 were injured, many with horrific burns but less than 10% of doctors and nurses in the city had survived and those few that were uninjured were very quickly overwhelmed. All communication with the city ceased abruptly, baffling the Japanese authorities. It was as if the city was no longer there.

Now Truman spoke, warning the Japanese there would be no compromise. Sixteen hours after the attack, he addressed the American people on the radio, saying:

'Sixteen hours ago an American airplane dropped one bomb on Hiroshima. It is an atomic bomb. We are now prepared to obliterate more rapidly and completely every productive enterprise the Japanese have above ground in any city. If they do not now accept our terms they may expect a rain of ruin from the air the like of which has never been seen on this earth."'

The Japanese ignored him. Within 48 hours, their own scientists had confirmed that Hiroshima had indeed been obliterated by an atomic bomb. The weapon was real, viable and lethal. How many did the Americans possess? Japanese experts told their leaders that it was probably only two or three – and that those others might not be ready yet. The Japanese leadership took the decision to brace themselves for more atomic strikes and to hold on.

Meanwhile, the Americans tried to crack the Japanese resolve. Leaflet raids told the Japanese people:

'We are in possession of the most destructive explosive ever devised by man. A single one of our newly developed atomic bombs is actually the equivalent in explosive power to what 2,000 of our giant B-29s can carry on a single mission. This awful fact is one for you to ponder and we solemnly assure you it is grimly accurate. We have just begun to use this weapon against your homeland. If you still have any doubt, make inquiry as to what happened to Hiroshima when just one atomic bomb fell on that city.

...EVACUATE YOUR CITIES...'

MAIN IMAGE: Enola Gay ABOVE LEFT: Enola Gay and crew members ABOVE MIDDLE: Little Boy on trailer cradle in pit on Tinian island, before being loaded into Enola Gay's bomb bay ABOVE RIGHT: 509th Composite Group aircraft immediately before their bombing mission of Hiroshima. Left to right: Back-up plane, The Great Artiste, Enola Gay

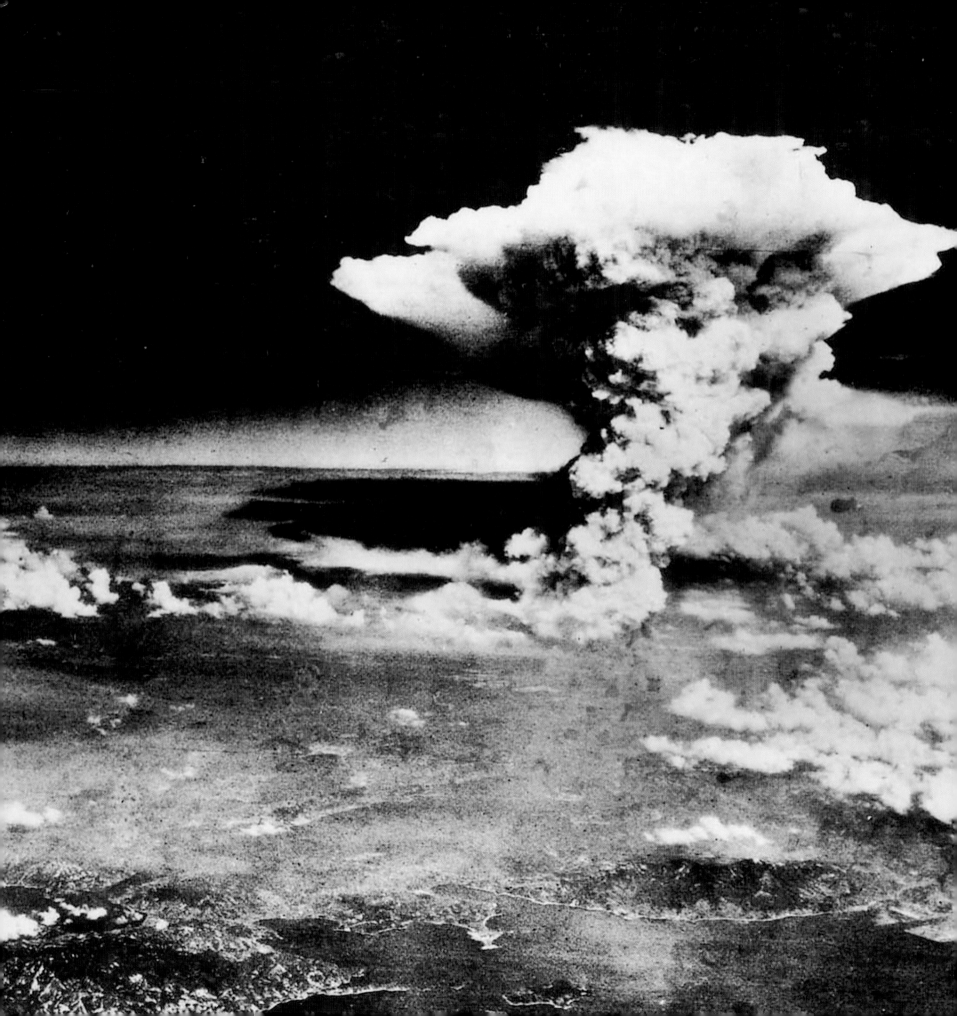

NAGASAKI

'I saw the atom bomb. I was four then. I remember the cicadas chirping. The atom bomb was the last thing that happened in the war and no more bad things have happened since then, but I don't have my Mummy any more. So even if it isn't bad any more, I'm not happy.'

Kayano Nagai, survivor

Just before 4 o'clock in the morning on August 9, the B-29 Bockscar took off from Tinian with a plutonium based atomic bomb codenamed Fat Man on board. Its target – Kokura. As it headed out, advanced B-29s flying weather report missions radioed in that conditions over the target were good. However, Bockscar had difficulties making a rendezvous with its two support and photographic B-29s, Big Stink and The Great Artiste. Only the latter of the two made the rendezvous and the mission was running 30 minutes late by the time the two aircraft reached Kokura. By then, weather conditions had severely deteriorated and visibility was hampered both by smoke from a nearby burning city and a deliberate Japanese smokescreen. Three times Bockscar made its bomb run over Kokura, under fire from Japanese anti-aircraft batteries, but each time the target proved invisible. Now there was talk of Japanese fighters coming in and – with Bockscar having already problems with a faulty fuel pump – the decision was made to abandon the strike and head for the secondary designated target instead. Nagasaki.

Bockscar and The Great Artiste reached Nagasaki just before 11am. At 11.02, the bombardier on board Bockscar was able to spot his target. They dropped Fat Man. The Bomb fell almost two miles off target. This time the inaccuracy mattered. Fat Man detonated in an air burst behind some hills, sheltering a significant part of the city from the blast. Fat Man was more powerful than Little Boy, but because the Bomb fell off target, casualties in the city were reduced. Nevertheless, 2.5 square miles of the city was destroyed. No one can give accurate figures but it's estimated that anywhere from 22,000 to 75,000 may have perished in the blast and the fire that followed. Uncountable others died of their injuries or from radiation poisoning in the days and weeks that followed.

America planned more nuclear strikes. There would be one more in August, then three more in September followed by three more in October…

MAIN IMAGE: Bockscar aircraft, which dropped an atomic bomb on Nagasaki **OPPOSITE PAGE; BOTTOM LEFT:** Fat Man on transport carriage, Tinian Island **BOTTOM MIDDLE:** Flight crew of the BocksCar. **BOTTOM RIGHT:** Dr. Norman Ramsey signing off the atomic bomb, Fat Man before it was dropped on Nagasaki

RUSSIA DECLARES WAR

Japan received a double hammer blow on August 9. Not only was Nagasaki destroyed but the Soviet Union also declared war on the nation. Over one and a half million Russian troops poured into Manchuria, slamming into Japan's Kwantung Army.

Some in the West saw this as little more than cynical posturing by Stalin and an attempt to make a land grab on Japanese territories but there is no doubt that the Japanese took the threat extremely seriously. They were facing invasion by the Western powers, their cities were being reduced to ashes and now a new, even more ruthless enemy was threatening them. Although today it is widely held that it was the two nuclear strikes that forced Japan to surrender, it's increasingly accepted in some quarters that Japan would have continued to resist even facing nuclear Armageddon and it was actually the threat of Russian aggression which made them finally realise that they had no hope. After all, one fire raid had probably killed more people in Tokyo than the strike on Hiroshima and the Japanese still didn't have a full appreciation of just what had hit their city. But a million and a half Soviet troops overrunning their forces in Manchuria was immediately comprehendible. It was thought that Soviets could be storming the beaches of the northern Home Island of Hokkaido in just over a fortnight – and the barbarous Stalin would certainly offer far less generous terms of surrender than the Western powers…

A DOUBLE BLOW

The Supreme Council were already in a meeting to discuss the Soviet entry into the war – and talk had turned to accepting the Potsdam terms – when they received the news about Nagasaki. They voted on peace terms and found themselves deadlocked. Those inclined to peace were happy to accept Potsdam but with extra guarantees about the Emperor's dignity. The more hawkish wanted changes that would mean Japan disarmed itself, dealt with any war criminals itself and would not allow a gaijin occupation.

As usual the meeting was held in hush tones behind locked doors. The Council had very real fears that, if the ordinary officers and men heard them discussing surrender, they would be murdered.

MAIN IMAGE: Operation August Storm, Soviet troops hoisted the flag of victory over the Harbin railway station, Manchuria, August 19, 1945
OPPOSITE PAGE; BOTTOM LEFT: Soviet marines are hoisting the banner in Port-Artur BOTTOM MIDDLE: The cabinet of Japanese Prime Minister Kantaro Suzuki BOTTOM RIGHT: Emperor Hirohito and General MacArthur, at their first meeting, at the U.S. Embassy, Tokyo, 27 September, 1945

FRUITS OF TORTURE

After Hiroshima, the Japanese had been quite desperate to know more about America's atomic capabilities. To this end they interrogated and tortured a captive Mustang fighter pilot, Lt. Marcus McDilda to learn more. Quite why they thought a humble fighter pilot would be privileged with such information is not known. McDilda told his horrified torturers that American possessed 100 atomic bombs (In reality it would have struggled to produce six) and what's more they were going to obliterate Tokyo and Kyoto in the next few days. The Japanese were so impressed by McDilda's insight that they let him live. He died at home in America in 2008.

McDilda's wild story went up the chain and was openly discussed by the Supreme Council. It gave them bitter food for thought.

JAPAN SURRENDERS

The Japanese authorities continued with a series of hasty meetings to discuss surrender but all were deadlocked. Eventually it was given over to the Emperor to decide. He chose surrender. By August 10 1945, Japan was announcing that it would accept Potsdam but that those terms could not *'prejudice the prerogatives'* of the Emperor. In other words, the Emperor would have the right of veto over any decisions the victorious Allies made. Two days later the Allies basically said we'll decide what the Emperor can or can't do. This threw the Japanese authorities - and their frantic debating was misinterpreted by the Allies as a sign that

they were preparing for an all-out fight to the finish instead. American bombing and shelling resumed. Once again, it was Hirohito who had the final say. Again he chose peace. Unconditional surrender it would be.

When word got out, extremist factions of the Japanese military attempted a coup d'état, seizing the Imperial Palace and attempting to murder Prime Minister Suzuki. He escaped the death squads sent for him by mere minutes. The coup failed when other units of the military refused to join in and remained loyal to the government. Rather than join the rebellion, War Minister Anami presented them with a dilemma by ritually disembowelling himself. The two leaders of the aborted coup then went out onto the streets, one on a motorbike and the other riding a galloping horse, and flung leaflets behind them explaining their motives. An hour later they both committed suicide.

At mid-day on August 15, the Emperor's surrender was broadcast on Japanese radio. Because Hirohito had chosen to give the script in an old, classical form of Japanese as befitted such a momentous occasion, a good number of his people couldn't understand what he was talking about. Others could – and many military men committed suicide there and then. Others chose to drag helpless American POWs out of their cells and cut them to ribbons with their katanas. The mass burning of sensitive documents began almost immediately, especially those relating to the small matter of war crimes.

By August 28 1941, American administrators had already flown in to begin the job of running Japan. Japanese civilian and military leaders signed the official surrender papers on September 2 on board the Battleship Missouri anchored in Tokyo Bay. Supreme Commander of the Allied Powers General MacArthur was there to accept the surrender – and in one of the battleship's staterooms hung the American flag that Commodore Perry had brought to Japan almost a century earlier. It was probably not coincidental.

There were more surrenders to come. The Japanese Command in South East Asia officially surrendered on September 12 at a ceremony in Singapore and Japan officially relinquished control of Formosa on October 25. The war in Manchuria between Japan and the Soviets did not end officially until 1956.

MAIN IMAGE: Japanese surrender signatories arrive aboard the USS MISSOURI in Tokyo Bay to participate in surrender ceremonies. September 2, 1945 **OPPOSITE PAGE; BOTTOM LEFT:** Rear Admiral Bazudi, Penang, signs the surrender document watched by the Japanese Lieutenant Governor of Penang (right) and the Admiral's chief of staff, Captain Hidakar **BOTTOM MIDDLE:** Sailors watch as Japanese surrender on board USS Missouri **BOTTOM RIGHT:** Vice Admiral Ruitako Fujita signing the Japanese Surrender of Hong Kong, 16 September 1945

THE TOKYO WAR CRIMES TRIALS

'War and treaty-breakers should be stripped of the glamour of national heroes and exposed as what they really are --- plain, ordinary murderers'

Joseph Keenan, chief prosecutor representing the United States

'At this place, the Japanese again started selecting prisoners to eat. Those selected were taken to a hut where their flesh was cut from their bodies while they were alive and they were thrown into a ditch where they later died'

Lance Corporal Hatam Ali

The International Military Tribunals for the Far East began hearing cases in Tokyo on May 3 1946. On trial were 28 members of the Japanese government and military. Almost two and half years later, the verdicts came in. 25 of the 28 were found guilty. Of the remaining three, two had died during the course of their trials and a third had been found insane.

Seven death sentences were handed down. The men included former Prime Minister General Hideki Tojo, Iwane Matsui (the commander during the Rape of Nanking) and Heitaro Kimura, who had committed particular atrocities against POWs. They were each hung on December 23 1948. Sixteen others were sentenced to life imprisonment. In other trials held outside Japan, a further 5,000 men were found guilty of committing war crimes. Just under 1,000 were executed.

Emperor Hirohito was not tried.

MAIN IMAGE: Hideki Tojo, former Japanese General Premier and War Minister, takes the stand for the first time during the International Tribunal trials, Tokyo **ABOVE LEFT:** Joseph Berry Keenan **ABOVE MIDDLE:** The defendants at the International Military Tribunal for the Far East Ichigaya Court **ABOVE RIGHT:** Class-A War Criminals in bus

THE LAST HOLDOUT

On February 20 1974, Second Lieutenant Hiroo Onoda was found living wild on the Philippine island of Lubang. His unit having taken heavy casualties in February 1945, Onoda had taken to the hills to hide. He had seen leaflets saying that the war was over, but hadn't believed them, so he kept on fighting and hiding for decades. A Japanese tourist found him, but Onoda still refused to surrender until given orders by his former commanding officer. The officer was still alive, successfully located and flown to the Philippines to officially relieve Onoda. Onoda surrendered his rifle, stash of hand grenades and the ceremonial suicide dagger his mother had given him should he ever be in danger of dishonouring himself.

Onoda received a hero's welcome on returning to Japan and there was even talk of him running for Parliament. Onoda found 1970s Japan mystifyingly soft and liberal and not at all to his liking. He ended up campaigning for a political return to Emperor Worship and military rule, whilst running a distinctly strange organisation for boys. He died in 2014, aged 91. In the West, people laughed and the Japanese soldier who doesn't know the war is over briefly became the staple fare of comedy television sketches.

While hiding out and refusing to believe the war was over, Onoda killed 30 local people.

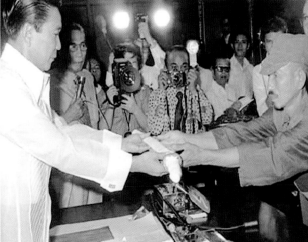

ABOVE LEFT: Hideki Tojo at the Japanese War Crimes Trials **ABOVE MIDDLE:** Hiroo Onoda (right) and his younger brother Shigeo Onoda **ABOVE RIGHT:** Japanese imperial army soldier Hiroo Onoda (R) offering his military sword to Philippine President Ferdinand E. Marcos (L) on the day of his surrender, March 11, 1974

ABOVE: former Japanese imperial army soldier Hiroo Onoda walking from the jungle where he had hidden on Lubang island in the Philippines